swoon
maine

by Carrie Bostick Hoge for madder

cover design by jennifer sarah muller

photography, styling, and interior book design
by carrie bostick hoge

isbn 9780997018400

10 9 8 7 6 5 4 3 2 1
published by Madder
printed in Maine

view from the bridge « bucksport, maine

table of contents

As I sat in my studio during the cold winter months earlier this year, I imagined several different project ideas. I wrote them down. Sat with each idea and pondered which should come first. I kept returning to a book dedicated to the natural beauty that I am surrounded by everyday. It seemed like the truest body of work I could create and that's where my heart wanted to be. Somewhere amazing, somewhere important, somewhere sincere. Maine. My muse.

Swoon!

I love you, Maine. You brought me my husband and two children. And, my backyard barn studio. You introduced me to Pam Allen, owner of Quince & Co. yarn company, from whom I have learned so many important lessons about knitwear design and life in general. Your light, Maine, always makes me smile. Your salty air smell and sometimes foggy mornings are magical. Maine, your forests are enchanting. You are always there to inspire me. So this book is my ode to Maine.

For this collection, I have designed 11 pieces, all with Maine in mind. The knits have a casual and easy-going style. The color palette for *Sea Pullover* and *Shore Cardigan* are inspired by just that— the deep blue of the water and the soft gray of the rocky shore. And *Shoreline Vest* is similar—with its green-gray that can be found on the rocks of the sea. A fair isle yoked pullover feels like a must-have Maine sweater and so *Lighthouse Pullover* was added. The color-work design was influenced not only by lighthouses, but also driftwood, shells, and sea stones.

The simple textures that appear in my accessories also have a casual style, but with a bit more knitting interest than the soothing stockinette stitch which appears in the garments. *Camp Cap*, created for Imogen during a visit to our family camp in the Moosehead Lake Region, features a mixture of broken rib and garter stitch. The cap set the tone for *Conifer Cowl* and *Maine Mitts* which both feature different variations of garter stitch ribbing, a favorite stitch pattern of mine. *South Paris Cowl* was previously released in Cecily Glowik MacDonald's ebook *Ashore*. For *Swoon*, I added a short version as well which takes half the yarn, and also, half the knitting time.

This book wouldn't be complete, to me, without sweaters for the litte ones. You'll find three sweaters for children, as well as the cap which includes sizes for kids. Growing up in Maine is special and I think having something hand-knit makes the experience that much more remarkable.

There are also 3 additional designs from a few friends. A comfortable and stylish cocoon cardi by Cecily Glowik MacDonald, inspired by the morning sky. A gorgeous shawl by Leila Raabe, influenced by the magnificent trees of Maine. And lastly, a pair of perfect mittens by Mary Jane Mucklestone, with a fair isle pattern that conjures her adoration of lichen on a favorite rock.

Living in Maine is a sweet gift. This state is a constant catalyst of creativity. If ever I need to be lifted up, I take a walk in the woods. I watch and listen to the birds and pick pinecones. Or, I take a short drive to be by the water's side. I smell the sea air, I hear the fog horn and gulls, and I close my eyes and dream...

I hope *Swoon* gives you a sense of why I love Maine, so you can dream this dream with me.

maine *made*

A local effort

To continue this devotion to Maine, I happily chose local talents and businesses when making this book. The yarns used in this collection are all from Maine based companies: Quince & Co., Swans Island, Peace Fleece, and Lana Plantae Yarns. The models are from Maine: my two daughters, Imogen and Sigrid, as well as Kate, Chloe, and Meghan. The book was printed locally at Franklin Printing in Farmington, Maine. The graphic designer who created this book's cover lives in Portland. Also, the tech editors, Kristen Ten-Dyke and Dawn Catanzaro, are local. Thank you for helping to make this book happen!

Friends of Madder swoon, too

There are some other fun little tidbits from my local friends. As I mentioned in the intro, you'll find one design from Cecily Glowik MacDonald, Mary Jane Mucklestone, and Leila Raabe, each inspired by living in Maine.

Bristol Ivy has a way with words, I've always known. So, I am pleased to include a short essay from her about what she loves about living here. Her very own ode to Maine.

I also asked the oh-so-talented knitwear designers, Pam Allen, Beatrice Perron Dahlen, and Hannah Fettig to contribute a few words that come to mind when they think about our beautiful state. In addition, they each shared a photograph or two that they took from one of their favorite places in Maine.

You'll also see a drawing by the prolific artist, Karen Gelardi, of plant-life in South Portland. I am thrilled to have it in *Swoon*, for her dedication to being a Maine artist is always an inspiration to me.

It is truly wonderful to have all these incredible contributions from some of the many talented artists and designers who live here in Maine.

maine knits
by carrie bostick hoge

kettle cove « cape elizabeth, maine

shore cardigan

sea pullover

maine mitts

brassua dam « rockwood, maine

mount kineo « rockwood, maine

little shore cardigan

kettle cove « cape elizabeth, maine

south paris cowl

kettle cove & two lights « cape elizabeth, maine

shoreline vest

long pond « rockwood, maine

little shoreline vest

tomhegan camp « rockwood, maine

33

little lighthouse pullover

lighthouse pullover

south paris cowl & *camp* cap

lighthouse road « stockton springs, maine

down a dirt road « rockwood, maine

camp cap

camp cap

marsh « portland, maine

building covered in vines & marsh « portland, maine

conifer cowl

brassua dam « rockwood, maine

swoon *maine*
{friends}

sunrise cardi *by cecily glowik macdonald*

marsh « portland, maine

tree shawl *by leila raabe*

kettle cove « cape elizabeth, maine

lichen mittens *by mary jane mucklestone*

two lights « cape elizabeth, maine

view from winslow park « freeport, maine

MAINE {love}

I've been asked multiple times what my favorite thing about Maine is, and each time my answer is different. The blueberry barrens, up north on the Airline to Canada, on a fall day when the sun is low enough to set the leaves ablaze. The marshes in Scarborough on a hazy evening when the tide is low and the light is golden. Autumn on the coast, when the smell of woodsmoke and leaf mold mix with the salt and tang of sea spray. The way the crooked brick sidewalks sound under my feet as I walk through my own neighborhood of Portland's West End. Every time I go around a cobblestoned corner, crest a hill on a winding back road, hear someone's lobster boat pass by in the distance in the chilly morning air, I fall a little bit more in love.

Because there is no one way to love this place. It manages to steal into your bones, to curl up there, and to surprise you with the ache of it when you least expect it. It is bittersweet and joyful and harsh and vibrant and lovely. It is a cacophony of adjectives, a whirlwind of moments and impressions and lives led. Maine is a place that encompasses all of these things, and yet at its core it remains still and calm and quiet.

I have no one way to explain how and why I love this place. But I know that, for all I may travel, for as long as I'm away, this little granite-y, stubborn, enduring bit of land will always be home.

Bristol Ivy

Resilient.

Hopeful.

Home is where you find yourself.

And if it has ocean views,
so much the better.

words & image: Pam Allen « *photo:* New Harbor, ME

quiet
tide
breath
rhythm
community

words & images: Beatrice Perron Dahlen « *photos:* Vinalhaven, ME

salty rocky dynamic folksy *home*

words & image: Hannah Fettig « *photo:* Jellison Cover in Hancock, ME,

drawing on carbon paper
by Karen Gelardi

the patterns

sea pullover
carrie bostick hoge

Finished measurements

31½ (35¾, 40, 44¼, 48½, 52¾, 57)" [80 (91, 101.5, 112.5, 123, 134, 145) cm] bust circumference

Shown in size 35¾" [91 cm] with 1¼" [4.5 cm] positive ease.

Suggested ease: 0-2" [0–5 cm] positive ease

Yarn

The All American Collection by Swans Island
(75% American wool, 25% American Alpaca;
80 grams / 210 yards [192 meters])

• 6 (6, 7, 7, 8, 8, 9) skeins in Atlantic

OR

1024 (1107, 1190, 1283, 1376, 1472, 1558, 1640) yards
[937 (1013, 1089, 1174, 1259, 1346, 1425, 1500) meters]
in heavy worsted weight yarn

Needles

• One 32" [80 cm] circular needle (circ) in size
  US 7 [4.5 mm]
• One 16" [40 cm] circ in size US 6 [4 mm]
• One set of double-pointed needles (dpns) in sizes
  US 6 [4 mm] and US 7 [4.5 mm]

Or size to obtain gauge

Notions

• Stitch markers
• Stitch holders or waste yarn
• Contrasting color waste yarn in similar weight for
  Sunday short-rows
• Tapestry needle

Gauge

17 sts and 26 rnds = 4" [10 cm] in stockinette stitch
with larger needles, after blocking.

Notes

Pullover is worked from the top down in one piece.
Sunday short-rows are worked to shape hem. Ribbed
hem is worked separately for front and back. Collar is
picked up and worked at the end.

Pullover

Yoke

With larger circ, and using the long-tail cast on, CO 49
(50, 51, 52, 53, 54, 55) sts. Do not join; work back and
forth in rows.

Begin stockinette stitch and place markers

First row: (WS) P2 for left front, pm, p8 for sleeve, pm,
p29 (30, 31, 32, 33, 34, 35) for back neck, pm, p8 for
sleeve, pm, p2 for right front.

Begin raglan shaping

Next row *raglan inc row:* (RS) *Knit to one st before m,
m1-R, k1, sl m, k1, m1-L; rep from * three more times,
knit to end (8 sts inc'd)—57 (58, 59, 60, 61, 62, 63) sts.

Next row: Purl.

Rep the last 2 rows one more time—65 (66, 67, 68, 69,
70, 71) sts; 4 sts each front, 12 sts each sleeve and
33 (34, 35, 36, 37, 38, 39) sts for back.

Begin raglan and neck shaping

Next row *neck and raglan inc row:* (RS) K2, m1-L, *knit
to one st before m, m1-R, k1, sl m, k1, m1-L; rep from
* three more times, knit to last 2 sts, m1-R, k2 (10 sts
inc'd)—75 (76, 77, 78, 79, 80, 81) sts.

Next row: Purl.

Next row *raglan inc row:* (RS) *Knit to one st before m,
m1-R, k1, sl m, k1, m1-L; rep from * three more times,
knit to end (8 sts inc'd)—83 (84, 85, 86, 87, 88, 89) sts.

Next row: Purl.

Rep the last 4 rows 1 (1, 2, 2, 3, 3, 3) more times—
101 (102, 121, 122, 141, 142, 143) sts; 10 (10, 13, 13, 16, 16,
16) sts each front, 20 (20, 24, 24, 28, 28, 28) sts each
sleeve and 41 (42, 47, 48, 53, 54, 55) sts for back.

Next row *neck and raglan inc row:* (RS) K2, m1-L, *knit to one st before m, m1-R, k1, sl m, k1, m1-L; rep from * three more times, knit to last st, m1-R, k2 (10 sts inc'd)—111 (112, 131, 132, 151, 152, 513) sts; 12 (12, 15, 15, 18, 18, 18) sts each front, 22 (22, 26, 26, 30, 30, 30) sts each sleeve and 43 (44, 49, 50, 55, 56, 57) sts for back.
Next row: Purl.

Cast on for neck
Next row *raglan inc row and neck CO:* (RS) *Knit to one st before m, m1-R, k1, sl m, k1, m1-L; rep from * three more times, knit to end, then using the backward loop cast on, CO 2 sts (10 sts inc'd)—121 (122, 141, 142, 161, 162, 163) sts.
Next row: (WS) Purl to end, then using the backward loop cast on, CO 2 sts—123 (124, 143, 144, 163, 164, 165) sts; 15 (15, 18, 18, 21, 21, 21) sts each front; 24 (24, 28, 28, 32, 32, 32) sts each sleeve and 45 (46, 51, 52, 57, 58, 59) sts for back.

Next row *raglan inc row and neck CO:* (RS) *Knit to one st before m, m1-R, k1, sl m, k1, m1-L; rep from * three more times, knit to end, then using the backward loop cast on, CO 15 (16, 15, 16, 15, 16, 17) sts. Do not turn, join to begin working in the rnd, then knit to m at end of left front. This is the new BOR (it might be helpful to change m to a different color) [23 (24, 23, 24, 23, 24, 25) sts inc'd]—146 (148, 166, 168, 186, 188, 190) sts; 47 (48, 53, 54, 59, 60, 61) sts each back and front, 26 (26, 30, 30, 34, 34, 34) sts each sleeve.

Cont raglan shaping
Next rnd: Knit.
Next rnd *raglan inc rnd:* *K1, m1-L, knit to one st before next m, m1-R, k1, sl m; rep from * three more times (8 sts inc'd)—154 (156, 174, 176, 194, 196, 198) sts.
Rep the last 2 rnds 3 (8, 6, 5, 2, 1, 0) more times— 178 (220, 222, 216, 210, 204, 198) sts; 55 (66, 67, 66, 65, 64, 63) sts each back and front, 34 (44, 44, 42, 40, 38, 36) sts each sleeve

Sizes - (-, 40, 44¼, 48½, 52¾, 57)" only:
Next rnd: Knit.
Next rnd *body inc rnd:* *Knit across sleeve to next m, sl m, k1, m1-L, knit to one st before next m, m1-R, k1, sl m; rep from * one more time (4 sts inc'd)— - (-, 226, 220, 214, 208, 202) sts.
Next rnd: Knit.
Next rnd *raglan inc rnd:* *K1, m1-L, knit to one st before next m, m1-R, k1, sl m; rep from * three more times (8 sts inc'd)— - (-, 234, 228, 222, 216, 210) sts.
Rep the last 4 rnds - (-, 1, 3, 5, 7, 9) more times— - (-, 246, 264, 282, 300, 318) sts; - (-, 75, 82, 89, 96, 103) sts each back and front, - (-, 48, 50, 52, 54, 56) sts each sleeve.

Size 31½ (-, -, -, -, -, -)" only:
Next rnd: Knit.
Next rnd *sleeve inc rnd:* *K1, m1-L, knit to one st before next m, m1-R, k1, sl m, knit to next m, sl m; rep from * one more time (4 sts inc'd)— 182 sts.
Next rnd: Knit.
Next rnd *raglan inc rnd:* *K1, m1-L, knit to one st before next m, m1-R, k1, sl m; rep from * three more times (8 sts inc'd)— 190 sts.
Rep the last 4 rnds 2 more times—214 sts; 61 sts each back and front, 46 sts each sleeve.

Size - (35¾, -, -, -, -, -)" only:
Next 3 rnds: Knit.
Next rnd *raglan inc rnd:* *K1, m1-L, knit to one st before next m, m1-R, k1, sl m; rep from * three more times (8 sts inc'd)—228 sts; 68 sts each back and front, 46 sts for each sleeve.

All Sizes:
Knit 2 (2, 2, 0, 0, 0, 0) rnds even.

Separate body and sleeve stitches, CO for underarm
Next rnd: Transfer 46 (46, 48, 50, 52, 54, 56) sts for sleeve to waste yarn or st holder, removing markers, using the backward loop cast on, CO 3 (4, 5, 6, 7, 8, 9) sts, pm for new BOR, CO 3 (4, 5, 6, 7, 8, 9) more sts, knit to next m, transfer 46 (46, 48, 50, 52, 54, 56) sts for sleeve to waste yarn or stitch holder, removing markers, using the backward loop cast on, CO 3 (4, 5, 6, 7, 8, 9) sts, pm for side, CO 3 (4, 5, 6, 7, 8, 9) more sts, knit to end—134 (152, 170, 188, 206, 224, 242) sts.

Body
Cont in St st in the rnd until body meas 2¼" [5.5 cm] from underarm.

Begin side shaping

Next rnd *inc rnd:* *K1, m1-R, knit to one st before m, m1-L, k1, sl m; rep from * one time (4 sts inc'd)— 138 (156, 174, 192, 210, 228, 246) sts.

Knit 29 rnds.

Rep the last 30 rnds one more time, then rep *inc rnd* one more time—146 (164, 182, 200, 218, 236, 254) sts.

Cont in St st in the rnd until body meas 13" [33 cm] from underarm.

Begin short-row shaping

Short-Row 1: (RS) Knit across back to side m, sl m, k4, turn work, place a strip of contrast color (CC) yarn across working yarn as for a Sunday Short-Row.

Short-Row 2: (WS) Purl across back to BOR m, sl m, p4, turn work, place a strip of CC yarn across working yarn as for a Sunday Short-Row.

Short-Row 3: Knit to turning point (where CC yarn was placed), resolve short-row for a RS row, then k3, turn work, place a strip of CC yarn across working yarn as for a Sunday Short-Row.

Short-Row 4: Purl to turning point (where CC yarn was placed), resolve short-row for a WS row, then p3, turn work, place a strip of CC yarn across working yarn as for a Sunday Short-Row.

Rep Short-Rows 3 and 4 two more times.

Short-Row 9: Knit to turning point (where CC yarn was placed), resolve short-row for a RS row, then k2, turn work, place a strip of CC yarn across working yarn as for a Sunday Short-Row.

Short-Row 10: Purl to turning point (where CC yarn was placed), resolve short-row for a WS row, then p2, turn work, place a strip of CC yarn across working yarn as for a Sunday Short-Row.

Rep Short-Rows 9 and 10 four more times.

Short-Row 19: Knit to turning point, resolve short-row for a RS row, then k3, turn work, place a strip of CC yarn across working yarn as for a Sunday Short-Row.

Short-Row 20: Purl to turning point, resolve short-row for a WS row, then p3, turn work, yo, knit to end.

Next rnd: Knit to first short-row gap, resolve short-row for a RS row, knit to one st before next gap, sl this next st knitwise, sl yo purlwise, knit these 2 together, knit to end of rnd.

Hem band
Begin garter stitch

Next rnd: Purl.

Sizes 31½ (35¾, 40, -, 48½, 52¾, 57)" only:

Next rnd *inc rnd:* *K24 (41, 91, -, 36, 59, 127), m1; rep from * 5 (3, 1, -, 5, 3, 1) more times—152 (168, 184, -, 224, 240, 256) sts.

Size - (-, -, 44¼, -, -, -)" only:

Next rnd: Knit.

All Sizes:

Next rnd: Purl.

Separate for front and back and begin 2x2 rib
Back

Next row: (RS) K1, *k2, p2; rep from * to last 3 sts before side m, k3, place rem 76 (84, 92, 100, 112, 120, 128) sts onto waste yarn for front.

Cont working back and forth in rows on 76 (84, 92, 100, 112, 120, 128) back sts as follows:

Cont working even in 2x2 rib as est until rib meas 2¾" [7 cm], body meas 18¾" [47.5 cm], measuring from side seam marker to underarm, ending after a WS row.

Next row: (RS) Loosely BO all sts in pattern.

Front

Transfer 76 (84, 92, 100, 112, 120, 128) held front sts onto longer, larger circ and join yarn ready to work a RS row. Cont working back and forth in rows as follows:

Next row: (RS) K1, *k2, p2; rep from * to last 3 sts, k3. Cont working even in 2x2 rib as est until rib meas 2¼" [5.5 cm], body meas 18¼" [46.5 cm], measuring from side seam marker to underarm, ending after a WS row.

Next row: (RS) Loosely BO all sts in pattern.

Sleeves

Transfer 46 (46, 48, 50, 52, 54, 56) held sts from one sleeve to larger dpns and divide sts as evenly as possible between needles. Attach yarn and pick up and knit 3 (4, 5, 6, 7, 8, 9) sts in the first half of underarm CO sts, pm for BOR, pick up and knit 3 (4, 5, 6, 7, 8, 9) more sts in rem underarm CO sts. Join to begin working in the rnd—52 (54, 48, 62, 66, 70, 74) sts.

Begin St st

First rnd: Knit.

Cont in St st in the rnd until sleeve meas 2" [5 cm] from underarm.

Begin sleeve shaping

Next rnd *dec rnd:* K2, k2tog, knit to last 4 sts, ssk, k2 (2 sts dec'd)—50 (52, 56, 60, 64, 68, 72) sts.
Rep *dec rnd* every 16th (14th, 12th, 12th, 10th, 10th, 10th) rnd one time, every 14th (12th, 10th, 10th, 8th, 8th, 8th) rnd three times, then every 12th (10th, 8th, 8th, 6th, 6th, 6th) rnd 1 (2, 4, 4, 6, 8, 8) times—40 (40, 40, 44, 44, 44, 48) sts rem.

Cont even in St st in the rnd until sleeve meas 14" [35.5 cm] from underarm.

Change to smaller dpns.

Begin garter stitch

Next rnd: Purl.
Next rnd: Knit.
Next rnd: Purl.

Begin 2x2 rib

Next rnd: *K2, p2; rep from * to end.
Rep the last rnd until cuff meas 4½" [11.5 cm], sleeve meas 18½" [47 cm] from underarm.

Next rnd: Loosely BO all sts in pattern.

Work second sleeve the same as the first.

Finishing

Steam- or wet-block to measurements.

Collar

With RS facing, smaller circ, and beg at center back neck, pick up and knit 14 (15, 15, 16, 16, 17, 17) sts along first half of back neck, 8 sts along sleeve, 10 (11, 11, 12, 12, 13, 14) sts along selvedge edge of front neck, 19 (20, 19, 20, 19, 20, 21) sts along front CO sts, 10 (11, 11, 12, 12, 13, 14) sts along selvedge edge of front neck, 8 sts along other sleeve, 15 (15, 16, 16, 17, 17, 18) sts along back neck—84 (88, 88, 92, 92, 96, 100) sts. Pm for BOR and join to work in the rnd.

Begin garter stitch

Next rnd: Purl.
Next rnd: Knit.
Next rnd: Purl.

Begin 2x2 rib

Next rnd: *K2, p2; rep from * to end.
Rep the last rnd until neck band meas 4½" [11.5 cm] from pick-up rnd.

Next rnd: Loosely BO all sts in pattern.

Weave in ends. Block again if desired.

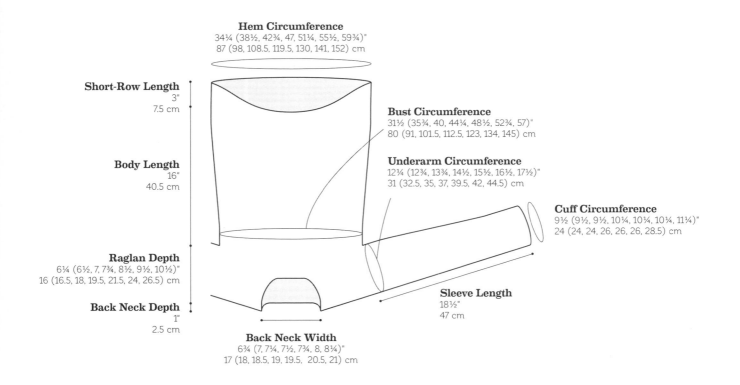

Hem Circumference
34¼ (38½, 42¾, 47, 51¼, 55½, 59¾)"
87 (98, 108.5, 119.5, 130, 141, 152) cm

Short-Row Length
3"
7.5 cm

Bust Circumference
31½ (35¾, 40, 44¼, 48½, 52¾, 57)"
80 (91, 101.5, 112.5, 123, 134, 145) cm

Underarm Circumference
12¼ (12¾, 13¾, 14½, 15½, 16½, 17½)"
31 (32.5, 35, 37, 39.5, 42, 44.5) cm

Body Length
16"
40.5 cm

Cuff Circumference
9½ (9½, 9½, 10¼, 10¼, 10¼, 11¼)"
24 (24, 24, 26, 26, 26, 28.5) cm

Raglan Depth
6¼ (6½, 7, 7¾, 8½, 9½, 10½)"
16 (16.5, 18, 19.5, 21.5, 24, 26.5) cm

Back Neck Depth
1"
2.5 cm

Sleeve Length
18½"
47 cm

Back Neck Width
6¾ (7, 7¼, 7½, 7¾, 8, 8¼)"
17 (18, 18.5, 19, 19.5, 20.5, 21) cm

shore cardigan
carrie bostick hoge

Finished measurements
32¾ (36¼, 39½, 43, 46¼, 49¾, 53, 56½)" [83 (92, 100.5, 109, 117.5, 126.5, 134.5, 143.5) cm] bust circumference, buttoned

Shown in size 36¼" [92 cm] with 1¾" [4.5 cm] positive ease.

Suggested ease: 0–2" [0–5 cm] positive ease

Yarn
Owl by Quince & Co. (50% American wool, 50% alpaca; 50 grams/ 120 yards [110 meters])
• 9 (10, 10, 11, 12, 13, 13, 14) skeins in Albertine
OR
1024 (1107, 1190, 1283, 1376, 1472, 1558, 1640) yards [937 (1013, 1089, 1174, 1259, 1346, 1425, 1500) meters] in worsted weight yarn

Needles
• One 32" [80 cm] circular needle (circ) in size US 7 [4.5 mm]
• One 16" [40 cm] circ in size US 6 [4 mm]
• One set of double-pointed needles (dpns) in sizes US 6 and 7 [4 and 4.5 mm]
Or size to obtain gauge

Notions
• Stitch holders or waste yarn
• Stitch markers
• Tapestry needle
• Seven ¾" [2 cm] buttons

Gauge
19 sts and 28 rows/rnds = 4" [10 cm] in stockinette stitch with larger needles, after blocking.

Notes
Cardigan is worked from the top down.
Circular needle is used to accommodate large number of sts. Do not join; work back and forth in rows.

Cardigan
Yoke
With larger circ and using the long tail cast on, CO 48 (52, 56, 58, 60, 62, 66, 68) sts. Do not join.

Begin stockinette stitch
First row *place markers:* (WS) P2 for front, pm, p7 (7, 8, 8, 9, 9, 10, 10) for sleeve, pm, p30 (34, 36, 38, 38, 40, 42, 44) for back neck, pm, p7 (7, 8, 8, 9, 9, 10, 10) for sleeve, pm, p2 for front.

Begin raglan shaping
Next row *raglan inc row:* (RS) *Knit to one st before m, m1-R, k1, sl m, k1, m1-L; rep from * three more times, knit to end (8 sts inc'd)—56 (60, 64, 66, 68, 70, 74, 76) sts.

Sizes 32¾ (36¼, 39½, 43, -, -, -, -)" only:
Next row: Purl.

Begin center front neck shaping
Sizes - (-, -, -, 46¼, 49¾, 53, 56½)" only:
Next row *raglan inc row:* (WS) *Purl to 1 st before m, m1-RP, p1, sl m, p1, m1-LP; rep from * three more times, purl to end (8 sts inc'd)— - (-, -, -, 76, 78, 82, 84) sts.
Next row *raglan and neck inc row:* (RS) K1, m1-L, *knit to one st before m, m1-R, k1, sl m, k1, m1-L; rep from * three more times, knit to last st, m1-R, k1 (10 sts inc'd)— - (-, -, -, 86, 88, 92, 94) sts.
Rep the last 2 rows - (-, -, -, 0, 0, 1, 2) more times— - (-, -, -, 86, 88, 110, 130) sts; - (-, -, -, 6, 6, 9, 12) sts each front, - (-, -, -, 15, 15, 20, 24) sts each sleeve and - (-, -, -, 44, 46, 52, 58) sts for back.
Next row: Purl.

All Sizes:
Next row: (RS) K1, m1-L, *knit to one st before m, m1-R, k1, sl m, k1, m1-L; rep from * three more times, knit to last st, m1-R, k1 (10 sts inc'd)—66 (70, 74, 76, 96, 98, 120, 140) sts.
Next row: Purl.

Rep the last 2 rows 5 (7, 8, 8, 7, 7, 6, 5) more times—116 (140, 154, 156, 166, 168, 180, 190) sts; 15 (19, 21, 21, 22, 22, 23, 24) sts each front, 21 (25, 28, 28, 31, 31, 34, 36) sts each sleeve and 44 (52, 56, 58, 60, 62, 66, 70) sts for back.

Next row: (RS) Using the backward loop cast on, CO 2 (2, 2, 2, 2, 3, 3, 4) sts, *knit to one st before m, m1-R, k1, sl m, k1, m1-L; rep from * three more times, knit to end [10 (10, 10, 10, 10, 11, 11, 12) sts inc'd]—126 (150, 164, 166, 176, 179, 191, 202) sts.
Next row: (WS) Using the backward loop cast on, CO 2 (2, 2, 2, 2, 3, 3, 4) sts, purl to end [2 (2, 2, 2, 2, 3, 3, 4) sts inc'd]—128 (152, 166, 168, 178, 182, 194, 206) sts.

Next row: (RS) Using the backward loop cast on, CO 3 (3, 3, 4, 4, 4, 5, 5) sts, *knit to one st before m, m1-R, k1, sl m, k1, m1-L; rep from * three more times, knit to end [11 (11, 11, 12, 12, 12, 13, 13) sts inc'd]—139 (163, 177, 180, 190, 194, 207, 219) sts.
Next row: (WS) Using the backward loop cast on, CO 3 (3, 3, 4, 4, 4, 5, 5) sts, purl to end [3 (3, 3, 4, 4, 4, 5, 5) sts inc'd]—142 (166, 180, 184, 194, 198, 212, 224) sts; 22 (26, 28, 29, 30, 31, 33, 35) sts each front, 25 (29, 32, 32, 35, 35, 38, 40) sts each sleeve and 48 (56, 60, 62, 64, 66, 70, 74) sts for back.

Cont working *raglan inc row* every RS row 10 (9, 10, 10, 8, 8, 7, 6) more times—222 (238, 260, 264, 258, 262, 268, 272) sts; 32 (35, 38, 39, 38, 39, 40, 41) sts each front, 45 (47, 52, 52, 51, 51, 52, 52) sts each sleeve and 68 (74, 80, 82, 80, 82, 84, 86) sts for back.

Sizes 32¾ (36¼, -, -, -, -, -, -)" only:
Next row: (RS) Work *raglan inc row* (8 sts inc'd)—230 (246, -, -, -, -, -, -) sts.
Work 3 rows even.
Rep the last 4 rows one more time—238 (254, -, -, -, -, -, -) sts; 34 (37, -, -, -, -, -, -) sts each front, 49 (51, -, -, -, -, -, -) sts each sleeve and 72 (78, -, -, -, -, -, -) sts for back.

Sizes - (-, 39½, 43, 46¼, 49¾, 53, 56½)" only:
Next row: (RS) Work *raglan inc row* (8 sts inc'd)— - (-, 268, 272, 266, 270, 276, 280) sts.
Next row: (WS) Purl.
Next row *body inc row:* (RS) *Knit to one st before m, m1-R, k1, sl m, knit to next m, sl m, k1, m1-L; rep from * one more time, knit to end (4 sts inc'd)— - (-, 272, 276, 270, 274, 280, 284) sts.
Next row: (WS) Purl.

Rep the last 4 rows - (-, 0, 1, 3, 4, 5, 6) more times— - (-, 272, 288, 306, 322, 340, 356) sts; - (-, 40, 43, 46, 49, 52, 55) sts each front, -, (54, 56, 59, 61, 64, 66) sts each sleeve and - (-, 84, 90, 96, 102, 108, 114) sts for back.

All Sizes:
Divide for underarm
Next row: (RS) Knit to m, transfer 49 (51, 54, 56, 59, 61, 64, 66) sts for sleeve to waste yarn or stitch holder, removing markers, using the backward loop cast on, CO 3 (4, 5, 6, 7, 8, 9, 10) sts, pm for side, CO 3 (4, 5, 6, 7, 8, 9, 10) more sts, knit to next m, transfer 49 (51, 54, 56, 59, 61, 64, 66) sts for sleeve to waste yarn or stitch holder, removing markers, use the backward loop method to CO 3 (4, 5, 6, 7, 8, 9, 10) sts, pm for side, CO 3 (4, 5, 6, 7, 8, 9, 10) more sts, knit to end—152 (168, 184, 200, 216, 232, 248, 264) sts on needle: 78 (86, 94, 102, 110, 118, 126, 134) sts for back, 37 (41, 45, 49, 53, 57, 61, 65) sts for each front.

Body
Cont to work in St st until body meas 2½" [6.5 cm] from underarm, ending after a WS row.

Begin side shaping
Next row *inc row:* (RS) *Knit to 2 sts before m, m1-R, k2, sl m, k2, m1-L; rep from * one more time, knit to end (4 sts inc'd)—156 (182, 188, 204, 220, 236, 252, 268) sts.
Rep *inc row* every 26th row two more times, removing side markers when shaping is complete—164 (180, 196, 212, 228, 244, 260, 276) sts.

Cont in St st until body meas 16" [40.5 cm] from underarm, ending after a WS row.

Begin short-row shaping
Short-Row 1: (RS) Knit to 5 sts before end of row, turn work, place one strip of CC yarn across working yarn as for a Sunday Short-Row.
Short-Row 2: Purl to 5 sts before end of row, turn work, place one strip of CC yarn across working yarn as for a Sunday Short-Row.

Short-Row 3: Knit to 3 sts before previous turning point (where CC yarn was placed), turn work, place one strip of CC yarn across working yarn.
Short-Row 4: Purl to 3 sts before previous turning point (where CC yarn was placed), turn work, place one strip of CC yarn across working yarn.
Rep Short-rows 3 and 4 four more times.

Short-Row 13: Knit to 4 sts before previous turning point (where CC yarn was placed), turn work, place one strip of CC yarn across working yarn.

Short-Row 14: Purl to 4 sts before previous turning point (where CC yarn was placed), turn work, place one strip of CC yarn across working yarn.

Rep Short-rows 13 and 14 four more times.

Next row: (RS) Knit to end of row and resolve short-rows as for a RS row.

Next row: (WS) Purl to end of row and resolve short-rows as for a WS row.

Hem band
Begin garter stitch
Next row: (RS) Knit.

Knit 3 more rows, ending after a WS row.

Begin 2x2 rib
Next row: (RS) K1, *k2, p2; rep from * to last 3 sts, k3.
Next row: (WS) P3, *k2, p2; rep from * to last st, p1.
Cont even in 2x2 rib until hem band meas 2" [5 cm], body meas approx 18" [45.5 cm], measuring from center back to underarm, ending after a WS row.

Next row: (RS) Loosely BO all sts in pattern.

Sleeves
Transfer 49 (51, 54, 56, 59, 61, 64, 66) held sts from one sleeve to larger dpns and divide sts as evenly as possible between needles. Attach yarn and pick up and knit 3 (4, 5, 6, 7, 8, 9, 10) sts in first half of underarm CO sts, pm for BOR, pick up and knit 3 (4, 5, 6, 7, 8, 9, 10) more sts in rem underarm CO sts. Join to begin working in the rnd—55 (59, 64, 68, 73, 77, 82, 86) sts.

Begin St st
First rnd: Knit.
Cont in St st until sleeve meas 2" [5 cm] from underarm.

Begin sleeve shaping
Next rnd *dec rnd*: K2, k2tog, knit to last 4 sts, ssk, k2 (2 sts dec'd)—53 (57, 62, 66, 71, 75, 80, 84) sts.
Rep *dec rnd* every 16th (12th, 10th, 8th, 8th, 6th, 6th, 6th) rnd 4 (4, 3, 6, 3, 11, 7, 3) times, then every 14th (10th, 8th, 6th, 6th, 4th, 4th, 4th) rnd 1 (3, 6, 5, 9, 3, 9, 15) times—43 (43, 44, 44, 47, 47, 48, 48) sts.

Cont even in St st until sleeve meas 14" [35.5 cm] from underarm.

Sizes 32¾ (36¼, -, -, 46¼, 49¾, -, -)" only:
Next rnd: K1-f/b, knit to end—44 (44, -, -, 48, 48, -, -) sts.

All Sizes:
Change to smaller dpns.

Begin garter stitch
Next rnd: Purl.
Next rnd: Knit.
Next rnd: Purl.

Begin 2x2 rib
Next rnd: *K2, p2; rep from * to end.
Cont in 2x2 rib until cuff meas 4½" [11.5 cm], sleeve meas 18½" [47 cm] from underarm.

Next rnd: BO all sts in pattern.

Finishing
Steam- or wet-block to measurements.

Neck Band
With RS facing and smaller circ, beg at hem edge of right front, pick up and knit 16 (18, 20, 21, 18, 19, 19, 20) sts along right front, 7 (7, 8, 8, 9, 9, 10, 10) sts along sleeve, 30 (34, 36, 38, 38, 40, 42, 44) sts along back, 7 (7, 8, 8, 9, 9, 10, 10) sts along other sleeve, 16 (18, 20, 21, 18, 19, 19, 20) sts along left front—76 (84, 92, 96, 92, 96, 100, 104) sts.

Begin garter stitch
First row: (WS) Knit.
Knit 2 more rows, ending after a WS row.

Begin 2x2 rib
Next row: (RS) K1, *k2, p2; rep from * to last 3 sts, k3.
Next row: (WS) P3, *k2, p2; rep from * to last st, p1.
Cont in 2x2 rib until neck band meas 1" [2.5 cm] (includes garter stitch rows), ending after a WS row.

Next row: (RS) Loosely BO all sts in pattern.

Buttonhole band

With RS facing and smaller circ, beg at lower edge of right front, pick up and knit 98 (98, 98, 100, 104, 106, 106, 110) sts evenly along right front edge.

First row: (WS) Knit.
Knit 4 more rows.

Next row *buttonhole row:* (RS) K3 (3, 3, 4, 3, 4, 4, 3), yo twice, k2tog, k13 (13, 13, 13, 14, 14, 14, 15)] six times, yo twice, k2tog, k3 (3, 3, 4, 3, 4, 4, 3) to end.

Next row: Knit to end, dropping second yo for each buttonhole.
Knit 3 more rows.

Next row: (WS) BO sts knitwise.

Buttonband

With RS facing and smaller circ, beg at neck edge of left front, pick up and knit 98 (98, 98, 100, 104, 106, 106, 110) sts evenly along left front edge.

First row: (WS) Knit.
Knit 9 more rows.

Next row: (WS) BO all sts knitwise.

Sew buttons opposite buttonholes.
Weave in ends.
Block again if desired.

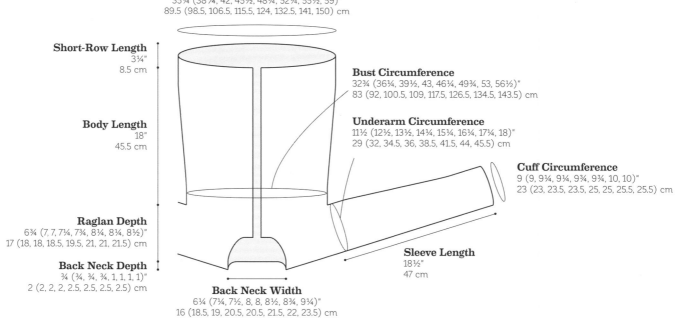

Hem Circumference
35¼ (38¾, 42, 45½, 48¾, 52¼, 55½, 59)"
89.5 (98.5, 106.5, 115.5, 124, 132.5, 141, 150) cm

Short-Row Length
3¼"
8.5 cm

Bust Circumference
32¾ (36¼, 39½, 43, 46¼, 49¾, 53, 56½)"
83 (92, 100.5, 109, 117.5, 126.5, 134.5, 143.5) cm

Underarm Circumference
11½ (12½, 13½, 14¼, 15¼, 16¼, 17¼, 18)"
29 (32, 34.5, 36, 38.5, 41.5, 44, 45.5) cm

Body Length
18"
45.5 cm

Cuff Circumference
9 (9, 9¼, 9¼, 9¾, 9¾, 10, 10)"
23 (23, 23.5, 23.5, 25, 25, 25.5, 25.5) cm

Raglan Depth
6¾ (7, 7, 7¼, 7¾, 8¼, 8¼, 8½)"
17 (18, 18, 18.5, 19.5, 21, 21, 21.5) cm

Sleeve Length
18½"
47 cm

Back Neck Depth
¾ (¾, ¾, ¾, 1, 1, 1, 1)"
2 (2, 2, 2, 2.5, 2.5, 2.5, 2.5) cm

Back Neck Width
6¼ (7¼, 7½, 8, 8, 8½, 8¾, 9¼)"
16 (18.5, 19, 20.5, 20.5, 21.5, 22, 23.5) cm

little shore cardigan

carrie bostick hoge

Finished measurements

19¼ (20¼, 22, 22¾, 23½, 26, 29½, 32, 34½)"
[49 (51.5, 56, 58, 59.5, 66, 75, 81.5, 87.5) cm] chest
circumference, buttoned

To fit sizes: 12 months (18m, 24m, 3 year, 4y, 6y, 8y,
10y, 12y)

Shown in size 23½" [59.5 cm] with 1½" [4 cm] positive ease
(right) and in size 19¼" [49 cm] with 1¼ [3.5 cm] (next page).

Suggested ease: 1-3" [2.5–7.5 cm] positive ease

Yarn

Owl by Quince & Co. (50% American wool,
50% alpaca; 50 grams/ 120 yards [110 meters])

• 3 (4, 4, 5, 5, 6, 7, 8, 9) skeins in Cerulean (blue) or
Sokoke (brown)

OR

337 (380, 460, 494, 539, 637, 764, 885, 1010) yards
[309 (348, 421, 452, 493, 583, 700, 810, 924) meters]
in worsted weight yarn

Needles

• One 32" [80 cm] circular needle (circ) in size
  US 7 [4.5 mm]
• One 16" [40 cm] circ in size US 6 [4 mm]
• One set of double-pointed needles (dpns)
  in sizes US 6 and 7 [4 and 4.5 mm]

Or size to obtain gauge

Notions

• Stitch holders or waste yarn
• Stitch markers
• Tapestry needle
• 4 (5, 5, 5, 5, 6, 6, 7, 7) ¾" [2 cm] buttons

Gauge

19 sts and 28 rows/rnds = 4" [10 cm] in stockinette
stitch with larger needles, after blocking.

Note

Cardigan is worked from the top down.

Circular needle is used to accommodate large number
of sts. Do not join; work back and forth in rows.

Cardigan

Yoke

With larger circ, using the long-tail cast on, CO 42 (42,
44, 42, 42, 42, 44, 44, 44) sts. Do not join.

Begin stockinette stitch

First row *place markers:* (WS) P3 (3, 3, 2, 2, 2, 2, 2, 2)
for front, pm, p8 (8, 8, 8, 8, 6, 6, 5, 4) for sleeve, pm,
p20 (20, 22, 22, 22, 26, 28, 30, 32) for back neck, pm,
p8 (8, 8, 8, 8, 6, 6, 5, 4) for sleeve, pm, p3 (3, 3, 2, 2,
2, 2, 2) for front.

Begin raglan shaping

Next row *raglan inc row:* (RS) *Knit to one st before m,
m1-R, k1, sl m, k1, m1-L; rep from * three more times,
knit to end (8 sts inc'd)—50 (50, 52, 50, 50, 50, 52, 52,
52) sts.

Next row: Purl.

Rep the last 2 rows one more time—58 (58, 60, 58, 58,
58, 60, 60, 60) sts; 5 (5, 5, 4, 4, 4, 4, 4, 4) sts each front,
12 (12, 12, 12, 12, 10, 10, 9, 8) sts each sleeve and 24 (24,
26, 26, 26, 30, 32, 34, 36) sts for back.

Begin front neck shaping

Next row: (RS) K2, m1-L, *knit to one st before m, m1-
R, k1, sl m, k1, m1-L; rep from * three more times, knit to
last st, m1-R, k2 (10 sts inc'd)— 68 (68, 70, 68, 68, 68,
70, 70, 70) sts.

Next row: Purl.

Rep the last 2 rows 2 (2, 3, 3, 3, 3, 4, 4, 4) more times—
88 (88, 100, 98, 98, 98, 110, 110, 110) sts; 11 (11, 13, 12, 12,
12, 14, 14, 14) sts each front, 18 (18, 20, 20, 20, 18, 20, 19,
18) sts each sleeve and 30 (30, 34, 34, 34, 38, 42, 44,
46) sts for back.

Next row: (RS) Using the backward loop cast on, CO 1 (1, 1, 1, 1, 2, 2, 3, 3) sts, *knit to one st before m, m1-R, k1, sl m, k1, m1-L; rep from * three more times, knit to end [8 raglan sts and 1 (1, 1, 1, 1, 2, 2, 3, 3) center front sts inc'd]— 97 (97, 109, 107, 107, 108, 120, 121, 121) sts.

Next row: (WS) Using the backward loop cast on, CO 1 (1, 1, 1, 1, 2, 2, 3, 3) sts, purl to end [1 (1, 1, 1, 1, 2, 2, 3, 3) sts inc'd for center front]—98 (98, 110, 108, 108, 110, 122, 124, 124) sts.

Next row: (RS) Using the backward loop cast on, CO 2 (2, 2, 2, 2, 3, 3, 3, 4) sts, *knit to one st before m, m1-R, k1, sl m, k1, m1-L; rep from * three more times, knit to end [8 raglan sts and 2 (2, 2, 2, 2, 3, 3, 3, 4) center front sts inc'd]—108 (108, 120, 118, 118, 121, 133, 135, 136) sts.

Next row: (WS) Using the backward loop cast on, CO 2 (2, 2, 2, 2, 3, 3, 3, 4) sts, purl to end [2 (2, 2, 2, 2, 3, 3, 3, 4) sts inc'd for center front]—110 (110, 122, 120, 120, 124, 136, 138, 140) sts; 16 (16, 18, 17, 17, 19, 21, 22, 23) sts each front, 22 (22, 24, 24, 24, 22, 24, 23, 22) sts each sleeve and 34 (34, 38, 38, 38, 42, 46, 48, 50) sts for back.

Cont working *raglan inc* row this next row, then every 4th row 1 (0, 0, 3, 2, 4, 3, 2, 3) times, then every 6th row 2 (3, 3, 1, 2, 1, 2, 3, 3) times—142 (142, 154, 160, 160, 172, 184, 186, 196) sts; 20 (20, 22, 22, 22, 25, 27, 28, 30) sts each front, 30 (30, 32, 34, 34, 34, 36, 35, 36) sts each sleeve and 42 (42, 46, 48, 48, 54, 58, 60, 64) sts for back.

Work 1 WS row even.

Divide for underarm
Next row: Knit to m, transfer 30 (30, 32, 34, 34, 34, 36, 35, 36) sts for sleeve to waste yarn or stitch holder, removing markers, using the backward loop cast on, CO 2 (3, 3, 3, 4, 4, 4, 5, 6) sts, pm for side, CO 2 (3, 3, 4, 4, 4, 4, 5, 6) more sts, knit to next m, transfer 30 (30, 32, 34, 34, 34, 36, 35, 36) sts for sleeve to waste yarn or stitch holder, removing markers, using the backward loop cast on, CO 2 (3, 3, 3, 4, 4, 4, 5, 6) sts, pm for side, CO 2 (3, 3, 3, 4, 4, 4, 5, 6) more sts, knit to end—90 (94, 102, 104, 108, 120, 128, 136, 148) sts.

Body
Cont working in St st until body meas 1 (1, 1½, 1½, 1½, 2, 2, 2, 2)" [2.5 (2.5, 4, 4, 4, 5, 5, 5, 5) cm] from underarm, ending after a WS row.

Begin side shaping
Next row *inc row*: (RS) *Knit to 2 sts before m, m1-R, k2, sl m, k2, m1-L; rep from * one more time, knit to end (4 sts inc'd)—94 (98, 106, 108, 112, 124, 132, 140, 152) sts.

Rep *inc row* every 18th (22nd, 10th, 10th, 10th, 10th, 14th, 22nd, 26th) row 1 (1, 1, 1, 1, 1, 2, 2) more times, then every 0 (0, 14th, 14th, 14th, 14th, 18th, 0, 0) row 0 (0, 1, 1, 1, 1, 1, 0, 0) times removing side markers when shaping is complete—98 (102, 114, 116, 120, 132, 140, 148, 160) sts.

Cont woking in St st until body meas 5½ (6, 7, 7, 7, 7½, 8½, 10¼, 11¼)" [14 (16, 18, 18, 18, 19, 21.5, 26, 28.5) cm] from underarm, ending after a WS row.

Begin short-row shaping
Short-Row 1: (RS) Knit to 5 sts before end of row, turn work, place one strip of CC yarn across working yarn as for a Sunday Short-row.
Short-Row 2: Purl to 5 sts before end of row, turn work, place one strip of CC yarn across working yarn as for a Sunday Short-Row.

Short-Row 3: Knit to 3 sts before previous turning point (where CC yarn was placed), turn work, place one strip of CC yarn across working yarn.
Short-Row 4: Purl to 3 sts before previous turning point (where CC yarn was placed), turn work, place one strip of CC yarn across working yarn.
Rep Short-Rows 3 and 4 four more times.

Short-Row 13: Knit to 4 sts before previous turning point (where CC yarn was placed), turn work, place one strip of CC yarn across working yarn.
Short-Row 14: Purl to 4 sts before previous turning point (where CC yarn was placed), turn work, place one strip of CC yarn across working yarn.
Rep the last 2 short-rows 2 (2, 4, 4, 4, 6, 6, 6, 6) more times.

Next row: (RS) Knit to end of row and resolve short-rows as for a RS row.
Next row: (WS) Purl to end of row and resolve short-rows as for a WS row.

Sizes 19¼ (20¼, 22, -, -, -, -, -, -)" only:
Next row *inc row:* (RS) K24 (25, 28, -, -, -, -, -, -), m1-L, k50 (52, 58, -, -, -, -, -, -), m1-R, k24 (25, 28, -, -, -, -, -, -) to end (2 sts inc'd)—100 (104, 116, -, -, -, -, -, -) sts.

Sizes - (-, -, 22¾, 23½, 26, 29½, 32, 34½)" only:
Next row: (RS) Knit.

All Sizes:
Hem band
Begin garter stitch
Next row: (WS) Knit.
Knit 2 more rows, ending after a WS row.

Begin 2x2 rib
Next row: (RS) K1, *k2, p2; rep from * to last 3 sts, k3.
Next row: (WS) P3, *k2, p2; rep from * to last st, p1.
Cont in 2x2 rib until hem band meas 1¼ (1¼, 1½, 1½, 2, 2, 2½, 2½, 2½)" [3 (3, 4, 4, 5, 5, 6.5, 6.5, 6.5) cm], body meas 6¾ (7¼, 8½, 8½, 9, 9½, 11, 12¾, 13¾)" [17 (19, 21.5, 21.5, 23, 24, 28, 32.5, 35) cm], ending after a WS row.

Next row: (RS) Loosely BO all sts in pattern.

Sleeves
Transfer 30 (30, 32, 34, 34, 34, 36, 35, 36) held sts from one sleeve to larger dpns and divide sts as evenly as possible between needles. Attach yarn and pick up and knit 2 (3, 3, 3, 4, 4, 4, 5, 6) sts in first half of underarm CO sts, pm for BOR, pick up and knit 2 (3, 3, 3, 4, 4, 4, 5, 6) more sts in rem underarm CO sts. Join to begin working in the rnd—34 (36, 38, 40, 42, 42, 44, 45, 48) sts.

Begin St st
First rnd: Knit.
Cont in St st until sleeve meas 2" [5 cm] from underarm.

Begin sleeve shaping
Next rnd *dec rnd:* K2, k2tog, knit to last 4 sts, ssk, k2 (2 sts dec'd)—32 (34, 36, 38, 40, 40, 42, 43, 46) sts rem. Rep *dec rnd* every 8th (12th, 8th, 10th, 10th, 26th, 26th, 26th, 26th) rnd 2 (1, 3, 3, 3, 1, 2, 2, 1) times, then every 0 (10th, 0, 0, 8th, 14th, 12th, 16th, 16th) rnd 0 (1, 0, 0, 1, 2, 1, 1, 3) times—28 (30, 30, 32, 32, 34, 36, 37, 38) sts rem.

Cont even in St st until sleeve meas 5 (5¾, 6, 7, 8, 10½, 12, 12½, 13½)" [12.5 (14.5, 15, 18, 20.5, 26.5, 30.5, 32, 34.5) cm] from underarm.

Change to smaller dpns.

Begin garter stitch
Next rnd: Purl.

Sizes 19¼ (-, -, 22¾, 23½, -, 29½, -, -)" only:
Next rnd: Knit

Sizes - (20¼, 22, -, -, 26, -, -, 34½)" only:
Next rnd *dec rnd:* K2, k2tog, knit to last 4 sts, ssk, k2 (2 sts dec'd)— - (28, 28, -, -, 32, -, -, 36) sts rem.

Size - (-, -, -, -, -, -, 32, -)" only:
Next rnd *dec rnd:* K2, k2tog, knit to end (1 st dec'd)—36 sts rem.

All Sizes:
Next rnd: Purl

Begin 2x2 rib
Next rnd: *K2, p2; rep from * to end.
Cont in rib as est until rib cuff meas 1¼ (1¼, 2, 2, 2, 2½, 2½, 3, 3)" [3 (3, 5, 5, 5, 6.5, 6.5, 7.5, 7.5) cm]; sleeve meas 6¼ (7, 8, 9, 10, 13, 14½, 15½, 16½)" [16 (18, 20.5, 23, 25.5, 33, 37, 39.5, 42) cm] from underarm

Next row: Loosely BO all sts in pattern.

Finishing
Steam- or wet-block to measurements.

Neck Band
With RS facing and smaller circ, beg at hem edge of right front, pick up and knit 9 (9, 10, 10, 10, 10, 11, 11, 11) sts along right front, 8 (8, 8, 8, 8, 6, 6, 5, 4) sts along sleeve, 20 (20, 22, 22, 22, 26, 28, 30, 32) sts along back, 8 (8, 8, 8, 8, 6, 6, 5, 4) sts along other sleeve, 9 (9, 10, 10, 10, 10, 11, 11, 11) sts along left front—54 (54, 58, 58, 58, 58, 62, 62, 62) sts.

Begin garter stitch
First row: (WS) Knit.
Next row: Knit.
Next row *dec row:* K1, k2tog, knit to last 3 sts, k2tog, k1 (2 sts dec'd)—52 (52, 56, 56, 56, 56, 60, 60, 60) sts rem.

Begin 2x2 rib
Next row: (RS) K1, *k2, p2; rep from * to last 3 sts, k3.
Next row: (WS) P3, *k2, p2; rep from * to last st, p1.
Cont in 2x2 rib until neck band meas 1" [2.5 cm], ending after a WS row.

Next row: (RS) Loosely BO all sts in pattern.

Buttonhole band

With RS facing and smaller circ, beg at neck edge of left front, pick up and knit 48 (53, 58, 58, 61, 65, 73, 83, 90) sts evenly along left front edge.

Begin garter stitch

First row: (WS) Knit.
Knit 2 (2, 2, 4, 4, 4, 4, 4, 4) more rows, ending after a WS row.

Next row *buttonhole row:* (RS) K5 (5, 6, 6, 5, 6, 4, 7, 8), *yo twice, k2tog, k11 (9, 10, 10, 11, 9, 11, 10, 11) rep from * 3 (4, 4, 4, 4, 5, 5, 6, 6) more times, yo twice, k2tog, k2.
Next row: Knit, dropping second yo for each buttonhole.

Knit 1 (1, 1, 3, 3, 3, 3, 3, 3) rows, ending after a RS row.

Next row: (WS) BO all sts knitwise.

Buttonband

With RS facing and smaller circ, beg at lower edge of right front, pick up and knit 48 (53, 58, 58, 61, 65, 73, 83, 90) sts evenly along right front edge.

First row: (WS) Knit.
Knit 5 (5, 5, 9, 9, 9, 9, 9, 9) more rows, ending after a RS row.

Next row: (WS) BO all sts knitwise.

Sew buttons opposite buttonholes.
Weave in ends.
Block again if desired.

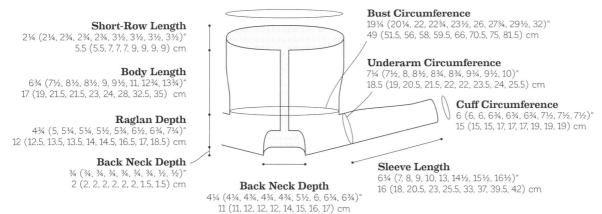

Hem Circumference
21½ (22¼, 24¾, 25¼, 26, 28¾, 30¼, 32, 34½)"
54.5 (56.5, 63, 64, 66, 73, 77, 81.5, 87.5) cm

Short-Row Length
2¼ (2¼, 2¾, 2¾, 2¾, 3½, 3½, 3½, 3½)"
5.5 (5.5, 7, 7, 7, 9, 9, 9, 9) cm

Body Length
6¾ (7½, 8½, 8½, 9, 9½, 11, 12¾, 13¾)"
17 (19, 21.5, 21.5, 23, 24, 28, 32.5, 35) cm

Raglan Depth
4¾ (5, 5¼, 5¼, 5½, 5¾, 6½, 6¾, 7¼)"
12 (12.5, 13.5, 13.5, 14, 14.5, 16.5, 17, 18.5) cm

Back Neck Depth
¾ (¾, ¾, ¾, ¾, ¾, ¾, ½, ½)"
2 (2, 2, 2, 2, 2, 2, 1.5, 1.5) cm

Bust Circumference
19¼ (20¼, 22, 22¾, 23½, 26, 27¾, 29½, 32)"
49 (51.5, 56, 58, 59.5, 66, 70.5, 75, 81.5) cm

Underarm Circumference
7¼ (7½, 8, 8½, 8¾, 8¾, 9¼, 9½, 10)"
18.5 (19, 20.5, 21.5, 22, 22, 23.5, 24, 25.5) cm

Cuff Circumference
6 (6, 6, 6¾, 6¾, 6¾, 7½, 7½, 7½)"
15 (15, 15, 17, 17, 17, 19, 19, 19) cm

Back Neck Depth
4¼ (4¼, 4¾, 4¾, 4¾, 5½, 6, 6¼, 6¾)"
11 (11, 12, 12, 12, 14, 15, 16, 17) cm

Sleeve Length
6¼ (7, 8, 9, 10, 13, 14½, 15½, 16½)"
16 (18, 20.5, 23, 25.5, 33, 37, 39.5, 42) cm

maine mitts
carrie bostick hoge

Finished measurements
7½" circumference at widest point of hand

Yarn
Lana Plantae Yarns (Local Maine alpaca fibers dyed naturally on their farm; 7 ounces [198 grams] / 200 yards [184 meters])

• 1 skein in Madder Root

OR

100 yds in heavy worsted weight yarn

Needles
• One set of double-pointed needles (dpns) in size US 7 [4.5 mm]

Or size to obtain gauge

Notions
• Waste yarn
• Stitch markers
• Tapestry needle

Gauge
16 sts and 26 rnds = 4" [10 cm] in garter stitch, after blocking.

Mitts
Using the long-tail cast on, CO 27 sts. Divide evenly among 3 dpns. Place marker (pm) for BOR and join to work in the rnd, being careful not to twist sts.

Begin garter stitch rib pattern
Rnd 1: *K1, p2; rep from * to end of rnd.
Rnd 2: Knit.
Rep the last 2 rnds for garter st rib pattern until rib meas 4" [10 cm] from the beg.

Begin garter st
Next rnd: Purl.
Next rnd: Knit.
Rep the last 2 rnds two more times.
Next rnd: Purl.

Begin thumb gusset
Set up rnd: K13, pm, m1-L, k1, m1-R, pm, knit to end (2 sts inc'd)—29 sts.
Work 3 rnds in garter st.
Next rnd *inc rnd:* Knit to 1st m, sl m, m1-L, knit to 2nd marker, m1-R, sl m, knit to end of rnd (2 sts inc'd)—31 sts.
Cont in garter st and rep *inc rnd* every 4th rnd two more times—35 sts; 9 sts between markers.

Divide for thumb
Next rnd: Purl to 1st marker, remove marker, purl to 2nd

marker, remove marker. Now, place the 9 sts that have just been worked onto waste yarn (these were the sts between your markers), then purl to end of rnd—26 sts rem on needles.
Next rnd: Knit until you reach held thumb sts, using the backward loop cast on, CO 1 st, then knit to end—27 sts. Work 5 rnds even in garter st, ending after a purl rnd.

Begin garter stitch rib pattern
Rnd 1: *K1, p2; rep from * to end of rnd.
Rnd 2: Knit.
Rep Rnd 1 one time.

Next rnd: BO all sts knitwise.

Thumb
Place held thumb sts onto needles.
Next rnd: Pick up and knit 2 sts, one on each side of backward loop cast on sts, on hand, knit to end—11 sts. Purl 1 rnd.
Next rnd *dec rnd:* K2tog, knit to end—10 sts. Purl 1 rnd.
Next rnd *dec rnd:* K2tog, knit to end—9 sts. Purl 1 rnd.

Begin garter stitch rib pattern
Rnd 1: *K1, p2; rep from * to end of rnd.
Rnd 2: Knit.
Rep Rnd 1 one time.

Next rnd: BO all sts knitwise.

Repeat for second mitt.

Finishing
Weave in ends. Steam- or wet-block to measurements.

south paris cowl

carrie bostick hoge

Finished measurements

Long version: 56" [142 cm] circumference and 8¼" [21 cm] width

Short version: 28" [71 cm] circumference and 8¼" [21 cm] width

Yarn

Finch by Quince & Co. (100% American Wool; 50 grams / 221 yards [202 meters])

• 6 skeins in Marsh for long version

• 3 skeins in Sedum for short version

OR in fingering weight yarn:

Long version: 1250 yards [1143 meters]

Short version: 625 yards [571 meters]

Needles

• One 16" [40 cm] circular needle (circ) in size US 4 [3.5 mm]

• One spare needle in size US 4 [3.5 mm]

Or size to obtain gauge

Notions

• Waste yarn

• Stitch markers

• Cable needle

• Tapestry needle

Gauge

33 sts and 37 rnds = 4" [10 cm] in Cable Pattern; after blocking.

25 sts and 38 rnds = 4" [10 cm] in Double Seed stitch, after blocking.

Abbreviations

C4B: (cable 4 back) Sl 2 sts onto cable needle, hold to back, k2, k2 from cable needle.

C4F: (cable 4 front) Sl 2 sts onto cable needle, hold to front, k2, k2 from cable needle.

Cable Pattern: (multiple of 8 sts)

(also, see chart page 82)

Rnds 1–3: Knit.

Rnd 4: *C4B, k4; rep from * to end.

Rnds 5–7: Knit.

Rnd 8: *K4, C4F; rep from * to end.

Rep Rnds 1–8.

Double Seed Stitch: (multiple of 4 sts)

Rnds 1–2: *K2, p2; rep from * to end.

Rnds 3–4: *P2, k2; rep from * to end.

Rep Rnds 1–4.

Notes

South Paris is worked in the round, lengthwise. Provisionally cast-on stitches are then grafted to the end, creating a tube.

Cowl

Using your preferred provisional cast on, CO 124 sts. Pm for BOR and join to begin working in the rnd, being careful not to twist sts.

First rnd *place markers and begin patterns:* P1, k1, pm, work Rnd 1 of Cable Pattern over next 64 sts, pm, k1, p1, pm, work Rnd 1 of Double Seed st to end.

Next rnd: P1, k1, sl m, work next rnd of Cable Pattern to next m, sl m, k1, p1, sl m, work next rnd of Double Seed st to end.

Work as est until piece meas approx 28 (56)" [71 (142) cm] from beg, ending after Rnd 8 of Cable Pattern.

Finishing

Remove waste yarn from provisional cast-on and place 124 sts onto a spare needle. Using the kitchener stitch, graft beginning of cowl to end of cowl, being careful not to twist.

Weave in ends. Steam- or wet-block to measurements.

south paris

cable pattern chart

					8
					7
					6
					5
					4
					3
					2
					1

KEY

☐ Knit on RS, purl on WS

⬡ C4B (cable 4 back): Sl 2 sts onto cable needle, hold to back, k2, k2 from cable needle.

⬡ C4F (cable 4 front): Sl 2 sts onto cable needle, hold to front, k2, k2 from cable needle.

shoreline vest
carrie bostick hoge

Finished measurements
30½ (33½, 35, 36½, 39½, 42¾, 45¾, 51¾, 54¾)"
[77.5 (85, 89, 92.5, 100.5, 108.5, 116, 124, 131.5, 139) cm]
bust circumference
Shown in size 35" [89 cm] with zero ease.
Suggested Ease: 0-2" [0–5 cm] positive ease

Yarn
Peace Fleece DK (75% Merino wool, 25% mohair;
113 grams [4 oz] /350 yards [320 meters])
• 2 (3, 3, 3, 3, 4, 4, 4, 4) skeins in Fathers Gray
OR
645 (712, 747, 781, 850, 926, 1000, 1067, 1143, 1221)
yards [590, 652, 685 , 715, 778, 847, 914, 976, 1046, 1117)
meters] in sport/dk weight yarn

Needles
• One 32" [80 cm] circular needle (circ) in size
  US 5 [3.75 mm]
• One 24" [60 cm] circ in size US 4 [3.5 mm]
Or sizes to obtain gauge

Notions
• Stitch markers
• Removable stitch markers
• Stitch holders or waste yarn
• Contrasting color waste yarn in similar weight for
  Sunday short-rows
• Tapestry needle

Gauge
21 sts and 31 rows = 4" [10 cm] in stockinette stitch
with larger needle, after blocking.

Notes
• Circular needle is used to accommodate large number
of sts. Do not join; work back and forth in rows.
• Vest is worked flat in one piece from the bottom up.
Sunday short-rows are worked to shape hem.

Vest
Hem
With larger circ and using the long-tail cast on, CO
172 (188, 196, 204, 220, 236, 252, 268, 284, 300) sts. Do
not join.

Begin 2x2 rib
First row: (WS) P1, *p2, k2; rep from * to last 3 sts, p3.
Next row: (RS) K3, *p2, k2; rep from * to last st, k1.
Cont working even in 2x2 rib as est until hem band
meas 3½" [9 cm], ending after a RS row.

Begin garter stitch trim
Next row: (WS) Knit.
Knit 2 more rows, ending after a WS row.

Begin St st
Next row: (RS) Knit.
Next row: Purl.

Begin short-row shaping
Short-Row 1: (RS) Knit to 6 sts before end of row, turn
work, place one strip of CC yarn across working yarn as
for a Sunday Short-Row.
Short-Row 2: Purl to 6 sts before end of row, turn work,
place one strip of CC yarn across working yarn as for a
Sunday Short-Row.

Short-Row 3: Knit to 3 sts before previous turning point
(where CC yarn was placed), turn work, place one strip
of CC yarn across working yarn.
Short-Row 4: Purl to 3 sts before previous turning point
(where CC yarn was placed), turn work, place one strip
of CC yarn across working yarn.
Rep Short-Rows 3 and 4 twelve more times.

Next row: (RS) Knit to end of row and resolve short rows as for a RS row.
Next row: (WS) Purl 1 row and resolve short rows as for a WS row.

Cont in St st until body meas 6" [15 cm] from beg, measuring along selvedge edge to exclude short-rows, ending after a RS row.

Next row *place markers:* (WS) P42 (46, 48, 50, 54, 58, 62, 66, 70, 74), pm, p88 (96, 100, 104, 112, 120, 128, 136, 144, 152), pm, p42 (46, 48, 50, 54, 58, 62, 66, 70, 74) to end.

Begin side shaping
Next row *dec row:* (RS) *Knit to 3 sts before m, ssk, k1, sl m, k1, k2tog; rep from * three more times, knit to end (4 sts dec'd)—168 (184, 192, 200, 216, 232, 248, 264, 280, 296) sts rem.
Rep *dec row* every 18th row three more times—156 (172, 180, 188, 204, 220, 236, 252, 268, 284) sts rem; 38 (42, 46, 50, 54, 58, 62, 66, 70) sts rem each front; 80 (88, 92, 96, 104, 112, 120, 128, 136, 144) sts rem for back.

Cont working even in St st until body meas 15" [38 cm] from beg, measuring along selvedge edge to exclude the short-rows, ending after a RS row.

Begin garter st armhole trim
Next row: (WS) *Purl to 8 (8, 8, 8, 9, 9, 10, 10, 11, 11) sts before side m, knit to m, sl m, k8 (8, 8, 9, 9, 10, 10, 11, 11); rep from * once more, purl to end.
Next row: (RS) Knit.
Rep the last 2 rows one more time, then work one more WS row as est.

Next row *underarm BO:* (RS) *Knit to 5 (5, 5, 5, 6, 6, 7, 7, 8, 8) sts before m, place the sts just worked onto a st holder or waste yarn, BO 10 (10, 10, 10, 12, 12, 14, 14, 16, 16) sts, removing m; rep from * one more time, knit to end—33 (37, 39, 41, 44, 48, 51, 55, 58, 62) sts rem each front and 70 (78, 82, 86, 92, 100, 106, 114, 120, 128) sts rem for back.

Cont working back and forth on left front sts only.

Left front
(Note: Read the following instructions before continuing. The neck shaping begins before the armhole shaping is complete.)
Continue garter st trim and begin armhole shaping
Next row: (WS) Purl to last 3 sts, k3.
Next row *dec row:* (RS) K3, k2tog, knit to end (1 st dec'd)—32 (36, 38, 40, 43, 47, 50, 54, 57, 61) sts rem.

Rep *dec row* every 4th row three more times, then every other row 2 (4, 5, 6, 7, 8, 9, 11, 12, 14) times; **and at the same time,** when armhole meas 1 (1½, 1¾, 2, 2½, 3, 3½, 3¾, 4¼, 4¾)" [2.5 (4, 4.5, 5, 6.5, 7.5, 9, 9.5, 11, 12) cm] from underarm BO, end after a RS row.

Begin neck shaping
Next row: (WS) BO 7 (7, 7, 7, 8, 8, 9, 9, 10, 10) sts, purl to last 3 sts, k3.
Next row: (RS) Knit.
Next row: (WS) BO 2 (2, 2, 2, 2, 3, 3, 3, 3, 3) sts, purl to last 3 sts, k3.

Next row *dec row:* (RS) Knit to last 4 sts, k2tog, k2 (1 st dec'd).
Rep *dec row* every 4th row three more times, then every other row four times.

When all armhole and neck shaping are complete you will have 10 (12, 13, 14, 15, 17, 18, 20, 21, 23) shoulder sts.

Cont working armhole in garter st trim as est and all other sts in St st until armhole meas 7¼ (7¾, 8, 8¼, 8¾, 9¼, 9¾, 10, 10½, 11)" [18.5 (19.5, 20, 21, 22, 23.5, 25, 25.5, 26.5, 28) cm] from underarm BO, ending after a WS row.

Begin shoulder shaping
Next row: (RS) BO 3 (4, 4, 4, 5, 5, 6, 6, 7, 7) sts, knit to end—7 (8, 9, 10, 10, 12, 12, 14, 14, 16) sts rem.
Next row: (WS) Purl to last 3 sts, k3.
Next row: (RS) BO 3 (4, 4, 5, 5, 6, 6, 7, 7, 8) sts, knit to end—4 (4, 5, 5, 5, 6, 6, 7, 7, 8) sts rem.
Next row: (WS) Purl to last 3 sts, k3.
Next row: (RS) BO rem sts.

Back
Return 70 (78, 82, 86, 92, 100, 106, 114, 120, 128) held back sts to larger circ and join yarn ready to work a WS row.

Continue garter st trim and begin armhole shaping
Next row: (WS) K3, purl to last 3 sts, k3.
Next row *dec row:* (RS) K3, k2tog, knit to last 5 sts, ssk, k3 (2 sts dec'd)—68 (76, 80, 84, 90, 98, 104, 112, 118, 126) sts.
Rep *dec row* every 4th row three more times, then every other row 2 (4, 5, 6, 7, 8, 9, 11, 12, 14) times—58 (62, 64, 66, 70, 76, 80, 84, 88, 92) sts rem.

Cont working armhole in garter st trim as est and all other sts in St st until armhole meas 7 (7½, 7¾, 8, 8½, 9, 9½, 9¾, 10¼, 10¾)" [18 (19, 19.5, 20.5, 21.5, 23, 24, 25, 26, 27.5) cm] from underarm BO, ending after a WS row.

Place removable marker on each side of center 34 (34, 34, 34, 36, 38, 40, 40, 42, 42) sts.

Begin shoulder and neck shaping
Next row: (RS) BO 3 (4, 4, 4, 5, 5, 6, 6, 7, 7) sts, knit to first m for right shoulder, join a second ball of yarn, BO center 34 (34, 34, 36, 38, 40, 40, 42, 42) sts, knit to end for left shoulder—9 (10, 11, 12, 12, 14, 14, 16, 16, 18) sts rem on right shoulder and 12 (14, 15, 16, 17, 19, 20, 22, 23, 25) sts rem on left shoulder.

Next row: (WS) BO 3 (4, 4, 4, 5, 5, 6, 6, 7, 7) sts, purl to end of left shoulder; on other side, BO 2 sts at neck edge, purl to last 3 right shoulder sts, k3—9 (10, 11, 12, 12, 14, 14, 16, 16, 18) sts rem on left shoulder and 7 (8, 9, 10, 10, 12, 12, 14, 14, 16) sts rem on right shoulder.

Next row: (RS) BO 3 (4, 4, 5, 5, 6, 6, 7, 7, 8) sts, knit to end of right shoulder sts; on other side, BO 2 sts at neck edge, knit to end of left shoulder—4 (4, 5, 5, 5, 6, 6, 7, 7, 8) sts rem on right shoulder and 7 (8, 9, 10, 10, 12, 12, 14, 14, 16) sts rem on left shoulder.

Next row: (WS) BO 3 (4, 4, 5, 5, 6, 6, 7, 7, 8) sts, purl to end of left shoulder sts; on other side, purl to last 3 right shoulder sts, k3—4 (4, 5, 5, 5, 6, 6, 7, 7, 8) sts on each shoulder.

Next row: (RS) BO 4 (4, 5, 5, 5, 6, 6, 7, 7, 8) rem right shoulder sts; on other side, knit to end of left shoulder.

Next row: (WS) BO 4 (4, 5, 5, 6, 6, 7, 7, 8) rem left shoulder sts.

Right Front
Return 33 (37, 39, 41, 44, 48, 51, 55, 58, 62) held right front sts to larger circ and join yarn ready to work a WS row.

(Note: Read the following instructions before continuing. The neck shaping begins before the armhole shaping is complete.)

Continue garter st trim and begin armhole shaping
Next row: (WS) K3, purl to end.

Next row dec row: (RS) Knit to last 5 sts, ssk, k3 (1 st dec'd)—32 (36, 38, 40, 43, 47, 50, 54, 57, 61) sts. Rep *dec row* every 4th row three more times, then every other row 2 (4, 5, 6, 7, 8, 9, 11, 12, 14) times; **and at the same time,** when armhole meas 1 (1½, 1¾, 2, 2½, 3, 3½, 3¾, 4¼, 4¾)" [2.5 (4, 4.5, 5, 6.5, 7.5, 9, 9.5, 11, 12) cm] from underarm BO, end after a WS row.

Begin neck shaping
Next row: (RS) BO 7 (7, 7, 7, 8, 8, 9, 9, 10, 10) sts, knit to end.

Next row: (WS) K3, purl to end.

Next row: (RS) BO 2 (2, 2, 2, 2, 3, 3, 3, 3, 3) sts, knit to end.

Next row: (WS) K3, purl to end.

Next row dec row: (RS) K2, ssk, knit to end (1 st dec'd). Rep *dec row* every 4th row three more times, then every other row four times.

When all armhole and neck shaping are complete you will have 10 (12, 13, 14, 15, 17, 18, 20, 21, 23) shoulder sts.

Cont working armhole in garter st trim as est and all other sts in St st until armhole meas 7¼ (7¾, 8, 8¼, 8¾, 9¼, 9¾, 10, 10½, 11)" [18.5 (19.5, 20, 21, 22, 23.5, 25, 25.5, 26.5, 28) cm] from underarm BO, ending after a RS row.

Begin shoulder shaping
Next row: (WS) BO 3 (4, 4, 4, 5, 5, 6, 6, 7, 7) sts, purl to last 3 sts, k3—7 (8, 9, 10, 10, 12, 12, 14, 14, 16) sts rem.

Next row: (RS) Knit.

Next row: (WS) BO 3 (4, 4, 5, 5, 6, 6, 7, 7, 8) sts, purl to last 3 sts, k3—4 (4, 5, 5, 5, 6, 6, 7, 7, 8) sts rem.

Next row: (RS) Knit.

Next row: (WS) BO rem sts.

Finishing
Sew shoulder seams. Steam- or wet-block to measurements.

Neck Band
With RS facing and smaller circ, beg at right front neck edge, pick up and knit 47 (47, 47, 47, 48, 49, 50, 50, 51, 51) sts evenly along right front neck, 38 (38, 38, 38, 40, 42, 44, 44, 46, 46) sts along back neck, and 47 (47, 47, 47, 48, 49, 50, 50, 51, 51) sts along left front neck—132 (132, 132, 132, 136, 140, 144, 144, 148, 148) sts.

Begin garter stitch
Next row: (WS) Knit.
Knit 2 more rows, ending after a WS row.

Begin 2x2 rib
Next row: (RS) K3, *p2, k2; rep from * to last st, k1.
Next row: (WS) P1, *p2, k2; rep from * to last 3 sts, p3.
Rep the last 2 rows until neck band meas 1¼" [3 cm] from pick up row.

Next row: Loosely BO all sts in pattern.

Buttonhole band
With RS facing, smaller circ, beg at lower edge of right front, pick up and knit 2 sts for every 3 rows—89 (92, 94, 95, 97, 100, 103, 104, 107, 109) sts.

First row: (WS) Knit.
Knit 4 more rows.

Place removable marker ½" [1.5 cm] down from center neck. Place 2 more markers 2¼" [5.5 cm] apart from each other.

Next row *buttonhole row:* (RS) *Knit to 2 sts before m, k2tog, yo twice; rep from * two more times, knit to end.
Next row: (WS) Knit to end, dropping second yo for each buttonhole.
Knit 3 more rows.

Next row: (WS) BO sts knitwise.

Buttonband
With RS facing, smaller circ, and beg at neck edge of left front, pick up and knit 2 sts for every 3 rows—89 (92, 94, 95, 97, 100, 103, 104, 107, 109) sts.

First row: (WS) Knit.
Knit 9 more rows.

Next row: (WS) BO all sts knitwise.

Sew buttons opposite buttonholes.
Weave in ends. Block again if desired.

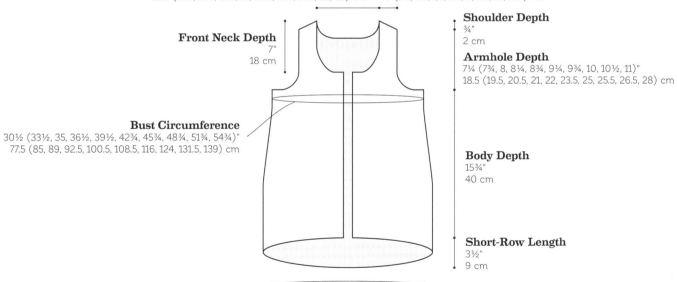

Back Neck Width
7¼ (7¼, 7¼, 7¼, 7½, 8, 8½, 8½, 8¾, 8¾)"
18.5 (18.5, 18.5, 18.5, 19, 20.5, 21.5, 21.5, 22, 22) cm

Shoulder Width
2 (2¼, 2½, 2¾, 2¾, 3¼, 3½, 3¾, 4, 4½)"
5 (5.5, 6.5, 7, 7, 8.5, 9, 9.5, 10, 11.5) cm

Front Neck Depth
7"
18 cm

Shoulder Depth
¾"
2 cm

Armhole Depth
7¼ (7¾, 8, 8¼, 8¾, 9¼, 9¾, 10, 10½, 11)"
18.5 (19.5, 20.5, 21, 22, 23.5, 25, 25.5, 26.5, 28) cm

Bust Circumference
30½ (33½, 35, 36½, 39½, 42¾, 45¾, 48¾, 51¾, 54¾)"
77.5 (85, 89, 92.5, 100.5, 108.5, 116, 124, 131.5, 139) cm

Body Depth
15¾"
40 cm

Short-Row Length
3½"
9 cm

Hem Circumference
33½ (36½, 38, 39½, 42¾, 45¾, 48¾, 51¾, 54¾, 58)"
85 (92.5, 96.5, 100.5, 108.5, 116, 124, 131.5, 139, 147.5) cm

little shoreline vest
carrie bostick hoge

Finished measurements
18 (18¾, 19, 20¼, 21¼, 22, 23½, 25½, 27)"
[45.5 (47.5, 48.5, 51.5, 54, 56, 59.5, 65, 68.5) cm] chest circumference
To fit size: 3 month (6m, 12m, 18m, 24m, 3 year, 4y, 6y, 8y)
Shown in size 19" [48.5 cm] with 1" [2.5 cm] positive ease.
Suggested ease: 1-3" [2.5–7.5 cm] positive ease

Yarn
Peace Fleece DK (75% Merino wool, 25% mohair; 113 grams [4 oz] /350 yards [320 meters])
• 1 (1, 1, 1, 1, 2, 2, 2, 2) skeins in Mourning Dove
OR
202 (220, 242, 280, 315, 337, 376, 443, 512) yards [185 (202, 222, 257, 289, 309, 344, 406, 469) meters] in sport/dk weight yarn

Needles
• One 24" circular needle (circ) in sizes US 4 and US 5 [3.5 and 3.75 mm]
Or size to obtain gauge

Notions
• Stitch markers
• Removable stitch markers
• Stitch holders or waste yarn
• Contrasting color waste yarn in similar weight for Sunday short-rows
• Tapestry needle

Gauge
21 sts and 31 rows = 4" [10 cm] in stockinette stitch with larger needle, after blocking.

Notes
• Circular needle is used to accommodate large number of sts. Do not join; work back and forth in rows.
• Vest is worked flat in one piece from the bottom up. Sunday short-rows are worked to shape hem.

Vest
Hem
With longer circ and using the long-tail cast on, CO 104 (108, 112, 120, 124, 128, 136, 148, 156) sts. Do not join.

Begin 2x2 rib
First row: (WS) P1, *p2, k2; rep from * to last 3 sts, p3.
Next row: (RS) K3, *p2, k2; rep from * to last st, k1.
Cont working even in 2x2 rib as est until hem band meas 1¼" [3.5 cm], ending after a RS row.

Begin garter stitch trim
Sizes - (-, 19, -, 21¼, 22, 23½, -, -)" only:
Next row: (WS) Knit.

Sizes 18 (18¾, -, 20¼, -, -, -, 25½, 27)" only:
Next row *dec row:* (WS) *K33 (35, -, 39, -, -, -, 48, 51), k2tog; rep from * one more time, knit to end— 102 (106, -, 118, -, -, -, 146, 154) sts rem

All Sizes:
Knit 2 more rows, ending after a WS row.

Begin St st
Next row: (RS) Knit.
Next row: Purl.

Begin short-row shaping
Short-Row 1: (RS) Knit to 4 sts before end of row, turn work, place one strip of CC yarn across working yarn as for a Sunday Short-Row.
Short-Row 2: Purl to 4 sts before end of row, turn work, place one strip of CC yarn across working yarn as for a Sunday Short-Row.

Short-Row 3: Knit to 2 sts before previous turning point (where CC yarn was placed), turn work, place one strip of CC yarn across working yarn.
Short-Row 4: Purl to 2 sts before previous turning point (where CC yarn was placed), turn work, place one strip of CC yarn across working yarn.
Rep the last 2 short-rows 5 (5, 7, 7, 7, 8, 8, 9, 10) more times.

Next row: (RS) Knit to end of row and resolve short-rows as for a RS row.
Next row: (WS) Purl 1 row and resolve short-rows as for a WS row.

Cont in St st until body meas 3¾" [9.5 cm] from beg, measuring along selvedge edge to exclude short-rows, ending after a RS row.

Next row place markers: (WS) P25 (26, 27, 29, 30, 31, 33, 36, 38), pm, p52 (54, 58, 60, 64, 66, 70, 74, 78), pm, p25 (26, 27, 29, 30, 31, 33, 36, 38) to end.

Begin side shaping
Next row dec row: (RS) *Knit to 3 sts before m, ssk, k1, sl m, k1, k2tog; rep from * three more times, knit to end (4 sts dec'd)—98 (102, 108, 114, 120, 124, 132, 142, 150) sts rem.
Rep dec row every 8th row 2 (2, 3, 3, 3, 3, 3, 3, 3) more times—90 (94, 96, 102, 108, 112, 120, 130, 138) sts rem; 22 (23, 23, 25, 26, 27, 29, 32, 34) sts rem each front; 46 (48, 50, 52, 56, 58, 62, 66, 70) sts rem for back.

Cont working even in St st until body meas 6 (6¼, 6¾, 7½, 8¼, 8½, 9, 10, 11)" [15 (16, 17, 19, 21, 21.5, 23, 25.5, 28) cm], measuring along selvedge edge to exclude the short-rows, ending after a RS row.

Begin garter st armhole trim
Next row: (WS) *Purl to 6 (6, 6, 7, 7, 7, 7, 8, 8) sts before side m, k6 (6, 6, 7, 7, 7, 7, 8, 8), sl m, k6 (6, 6, 7, 7, 7, 7, 8, 8); rep from * one more time, purl to end.
Next row: Knit.
Rep the last 2 rows one more time, then work one more WS row as est.

Next row underarm BO: (RS) *Knit to 3 (3, 3, 4, 4, 4, 4, 5, 5) sts before side m, place the sts just worked onto a st holder or waste yarn, BO 6 (6, 6, 8, 8, 8, 8, 10, 10) sts, removing side m; rep from * once more, knit to end—19 (20, 20, 21, 22, 23, 25, 27, 29) sts rem for each front and 40 (42, 44, 44, 48, 50, 54, 56, 60) sts rem for back.

Cont working back and forth on left front sts only.

Left front
Continue garter st trim and begin armhole shaping
Next row: (WS) Purl to last 3 sts, k3.
Next row dec row: K3, k2tog, knit to end (1 st dec'd)—18 (19, 19, 20, 21, 22, 24, 26, 28) sts.
Rep dec row every 4th row one time, then every other row 1 (1, 1, 1, 1, 1, 2, 2, 2) more times—16 (17, 17, 18, 19, 20, 21, 23, 25) sts rem.

Cont working armhole in garter st trim as est and all other sts in St st until armhole meas 1½ (1½, 2, 2, 2½, 2½, 2½, 2½, 2½)" [4 (4, 5, 5, 6.5, 6.5, 6.5, 6.5, 6.5) cm] from underarm BO, ending after a RS row.

Begin neck shaping
Next row: (WS) BO 2 (3, 3, 4, 4, 4, 5, 6, 7) sts, purl to last 3 sts, k3—14 (14, 14, 14, 15, 16, 16, 17, 18) sts rem.
Next row: (RS) Knit.
Next row: (WS) BO 2 (2, 2, 2, 3, 3, 3, 3, 3) sts, purl to last 3 sts, k3—12 (12, 12, 12, 12, 13, 13, 14, 15) sts rem.

Next row dec row: (RS) Knit to last 4 sts, k2tog, k2 (1 sts dec'd)—11 (11, 11, 11, 11, 12, 12, 13, 14) sts rem.
Rep dec row every 4th row one time, then every other row two times—8 (8, 8, 8, 8, 9, 9, 10, 11) sts rem.

Cont working armhole in garter st trim as est and all other sts in St st until armhole meas 3½ (3¾, 4, 4½, 4½, 4¾, 5, 5½, 6)" [9 (9.5, 10, 11.5, 11.5, 12, 12.5, 14, 15) cm] from underarm BO, ending after a WS row.

Begin shoulder shaping
Next row: (RS) BO 4 (4, 4, 4, 4, 4, 4, 5, 5) sts, knit to end—4 (4, 4, 4, 4, 5, 5, 5, 6) sts rem.
Next row: (WS) Purl.
Next row: (RS) BO rem sts.

Back
Return 40 (42, 44, 44, 48, 50, 54, 56, 60) held back sts to larger circ and join yarn ready to work a WS row.

Continue garter st trim and begin armhole shaping
Next row: (WS) K3, purl to last 3 sts, k3.
Next row dec row: (RS) K3, k2tog, knit to last 5 sts, ssk, k3 (2 sts dec'd)—38 (40, 42, 42, 46, 48, 52, 54, 58) sts.
Rep dec row every 4th row one time, then every other row 1 (1, 1, 1, 1, 1, 2, 2, 2) times—34 (36, 38, 38, 42, 44, 46, 48, 52) sts rem.

Cont working armhole in garter st trim as est and all other sts in St st until armhole meas 3½ (3¾, 4, 4½, 4½, 4¾, 5, 5½, 6)" [9 (9.5, 10, 11.5, 11.5, 12, 12.5, 14, 15) cm] from underarm BO, ending after a WS row.

Place removable marker on each side of center 18 (20, 22, 22, 26, 26, 28, 28, 30) sts.

Begin shoulder shaping
Next row: (RS) BO 4 (4, 4, 4, 4, 4, 5, 5) sts, knit to first m for right shoulder, join a second ball of yarn, BO center 18 (20, 22, 22, 26, 26, 28, 28, 30) sts, knit to end for left shoulder—4 (4, 4, 4, 4, 5, 5, 5, 6) sts rem on right shoulder and 8 (8, 8, 8, 8, 9, 9, 10, 11) sts rem on left shoulder.
Next row: (WS) BO 4 (4, 4, 4, 4, 4, 4, 5, 5), purl to end of left shoulder; on other side, purl to end of right shoulder—4 (4, 4, 4, 4, 5, 5, 5, 6) sts rem on each shoulder.
Next row: (RS) BO 4 (4, 4, 4, 4, 5, 5, 5, 6) rem right shoulder sts; on other side, knit to end of left shoulder—4 (4, 4, 4, 4, 5, 5, 5, 6) sts rem on left shoulder.
Next row: (WS) BO 4 (4, 4, 4, 4, 5, 5, 5, 6) 3 rem left shoulder sts.

Right Front
Return 19 (20, 20, 21, 22, 23, 25, 27, 29) held right front sts to larger circ and join yarn ready to work a WS row.

Continue garter st trim and begin armhole shaping
Next row: (WS) K3, purl to end.
Next row *dec row:* (RS) Knit to last 5 sts, ssk, k3 (1 st dec'd)—18 (19, 19, 20, 21, 22, 24, 26, 28) sts.
Rep *dec row* every 4th row one time, then every other row 1 (1, 1, 1, 1, 1, 2, 2, 2) more times—16 (17, 17, 18, 19, 20, 21, 23, 25) sts rem.

Cont working armhole in garter st trim as est and all other sts in St st until armhole meas 1½ (1½, 2, 2, 2½, 2½, 2½, 2½, 2½)" [4 (4, 5, 5, 6.5, 6.5, 6.5, 6.5, 6.5) cm] from underarm BO, end after a WS row.

Begin neck shaping
Next row: (RS) BO 3 (3, 4, 4, 5, 5, 6, 6, 7) sts, knit to end—14 (14, 14, 14, 15, 16, 16, 17, 18) sts rem.
Next row: (WS) K3, purl to end.
Next row: (RS) BO 2 (2, 2, 2, 3, 3, 3, 3, 3) sts, knit to end—12 (12, 12, 12, 12, 13, 13, 14, 15) sts rem.
Next row: (WS) K3, purl to end.

Next row *dec row:* (RS) K2, ssk, knit to end (1 st dec'd)— 11 (11, 11, 11, 11, 12, 12, 13, 14) sts rem.
Rep *dec row* every 4th row one time, then every other row two times—8 (8, 8, 8, 8, 9, 9, 10, 11) sts rem.

Cont working armhole in garter st trim as est and all other sts in St st until armhole meas 3½ (3¾, 4, 4½, 4½, 4¾, 5, 5½, 6)" [9 (9.5, 10, 11.5, 11.5, 12, 12.5, 14, 15) cm] from underarm BO, ending after a RS row.

Begin shoulder shaping
Next row: (WS) BO 4 (4, 4, 4, 4, 4, 5, 5) sts—4 (4, 4, 4, 5, 5, 5, 6) sts rem.
Next row: (RS) Knit.
Next row: (WS) BO rem sts.

Finishing
Sew shoulder seams.
Steam- or wet-block to measurements.

Neck Band
With RS facing, and beg at right front edge, pick up and knit 11 (12, 13, 13, 15, 15, 16, 16, 17) sts along right front, 18 (20, 22, 22, 26, 26, 28, 28, 30) sts along back neck, and 11 (12, 13, 13, 15, 15, 16, 16, 17) sts along left front—40 (44, 48, 48, 56, 56, 60, 60, 64) sts.

Begin garter stitch
Next row: (WS) Knit.
Knit 2 more rows, ending after a WS row.

Begin 2x2 rib
Next row: (RS) K3, *p2, k2; rep from * to last st, k1.
Next row: (WS) P1, *p2, k2; rep from * to last 3 sts, p3.
Rep the last 2 rows until neck band meas 1¼" [3.5 cm] from pick up row.

Next row: Loosely BO all sts in pattern.

Buttonhole band
With RS facing, smaller circ, and beg at lower edge of right front, pick up and knit 2 sts for every 3 rows—42 (43, 49, 52, 56, 58, 60, 65, 71) sts.

First row: (WS) Knit.
Knit 2 more rows.

Place removable marker ½" [1.5 cm] down from center neck. Place 2 more markers 1½" [4 cm] apart from each other.
Next row *buttonhole row:* (RS) *Knit to 2 sts before m, k2tog, yo twice; rep from * two more times, knit to end.
Next row: (WS) Knit to end, dropping second yo for each buttonhole.
Knit 1 more row.

Next row: (WS) BO sts knitwise.

Buttonband

With RS facing, smaller circ, and beg at neck edge of left front, pick up and knit 2 sts for every 3 rows— 42 (43, 49, 52, 56, 58, 60, 65, 71) sts.

First row: (WS) Knit.
Knit 5 more rows.

Next row: (WS) BO all sts knitwise.

Sew buttons opposite buttonholes. Weave in ends. Block again if desired.

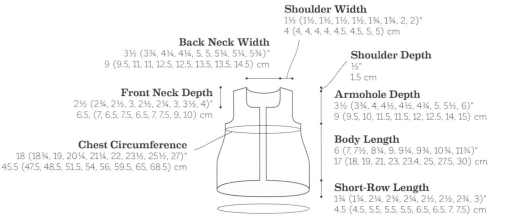

Shoulder Width
1½ (1½, 1½, 1½, 1½, 1¾, 1¾, 2, 2)"
4 (4, 4, 4, 4.5, 4.5, 5, 5) cm

Back Neck Width
3½ (3¾, 4¼, 4¼, 5, 5, 5¼, 5¼, 5¾)"
9 (9.5, 11, 11, 12.5, 12.5, 13.5, 13.5, 14.5) cm

Shoulder Depth
½"
1.5 cm

Front Neck Depth
2½ (2¾, 2½, 3, 2½, 2¾, 3, 3½, 4)"
6.5, (7, 6.5, 7.5, 6.5, 7, 7.5, 9, 10) cm

Armhole Depth
3½ (3¾, 4, 4½, 4½, 4¾, 5, 5½, 6)"
9 (9.5, 10, 11.5, 11.5, 12, 12.5, 14, 15) cm

Chest Circumference
18 (18¾, 19, 20¼, 21¼, 22, 23½, 25½, 27)"
45.5 (47.5, 48.5, 51.5, 54, 56, 59.5, 65, 68.5) cm

Body Length
6 (7, 7½, 8¼, 9, 9¼, 9¾, 10¾, 11¾)"
17 (18, 19, 21, 23, 23.4, 25, 27.5, 30) cm

Short-Row Length
1¾ (1¾, 2¼, 2¼, 2¼, 2½, 2½, 2¾, 3)"
4.5 (4.5, 5.5, 5.5, 5.5, 6.5, 6.5, 7, 7.5) cm

Hem Circumference
20½ (21¼, 22, 23½, 24½, 25¼, 26¾, 29, 30½)"
52 (54, 56, 59.5, 62, 64, 68, 73.5, 77.5) cm

little lighthouse pullover
carrie bostick hoge

Finished measurements
22¼ (23½, 24¾, 27, 28¾, 30, 31½)" [56.5 (59.5, 63, 68.5, 75.5, 76, 80) cm] chest circumference
To fit sizes: 2 (3, 4, 6, 8, 10, 12) years
Shown in size 24¾" [63 cm] with 3" [7.5 cm] positive ease.
Suggested ease: 1–3" [2.5–7.5 cm] positive ease

Yarn
Lark by Quince & Co. (100% American wool; 50 grams / 134 yards [123 meters])
• 4 (4, 5, 5, 6, 7, 7) skeins Kumlien's Gull (Color A)
• 1 skein Honey (Color B)
• 1 skein Clay (Color C)
• 1 skein Bird's Egg (Color D)
OR in worsted weight yarn:
• 434 (481, 520, 619, 717, 817, 907) yds [397 (440, 476, 567, 656, 748, 830) meters] Color A
• 8 (9, 9, 11, 13, 14, 16) yards [8 (9, 9, 11, 12, 13, 15) meters] Color B
• 18 (20, 21, 25, 29, 33, 36) yards [17 (19, 20, 23, 27, 31, 33) meters Color C
• 8 (9, 9, 11, 13, 14, 16) yards [8 (9, 9, 11, 12, 13, 15) meters] Color D

Needles
• One 16" [40 cm] and 24" [60 cm] circular needle (circ) in size US 7 [4.5 mm]
• One 16" [40 cm] circ in size US 6 [4 mm]
• One set of double-pointed needles (dpns) in size US 7 [4.5 mm]
Or size to obtain gauge

Notions
• Stitch markers
• Stitch holders or waste yarn
• Tapestry needle

Gauge
19 sts and 28 rnds = 4" [10 cm] in stockinette stitch with larger needles, after blocking.

Notes
On Chart Rnds 13–20, the 4th stitch has been decreased and is not worked; on Rnds 21–23, the 3rd and 4th stitches have been decreased and are not worked.

Pullover
Body
With Color A, larger, longer circ, and using the long-tail cast on, CO 106 (112, 118, 128, 136, 142, 150) sts. Pm for BOR and join to work in the rnd, being careful not to twist sts.

Begin 1x1 rib
First rnd: *K1, p1; rep from * to end.
Rep the last rnd until rib meas 2 (2, 2½, 2½, 2½, 3, 3)" [5 (5, 6.5, 6.5, 6.5, 7.5, 7.5) cm] from beg.

Begin St st, place markers for side, cont with Color A
Work in St st in the rnd until body meas 8 (8½, 9, 9½, 10½, 12, 13)" [20.5 (21.5, 23, 24, 26.5, 30.5, 33) cm] from beg.
Next rnd: K53 (56, 59, 64, 68, 71, 75), pm for side, knit to end.

Separate for underarm
Next rnd: K3 (3, 4, 4, 4, 5, 5), sl the last 6 (6, 8, 8, 8, 10, 10) sts to st holder or waste yarn, removing BOR m, knit to side m, k3 (3, 4, 4, 4, 5, 5), sl the last 6 (6, 8, 8, 8, 10, 10) sts to st holder or waste yarn, removing side m, knit to end—47 (50, 51, 56, 60, 61, 65) sts rem each back and front.

Keep sts on circ and set aside. Do not break yarn.

Sleeves

With Color A, dpns, and using the long-tail cast on, CO 32 (34, 34, 36, 36, 38, 38) sts. Pm for BOR and join to work in the rnd, being careful not to twist sts.

Begin 1x1 rib

First rnd: *K1, p1; rep from * to end.
Rep the last rnd until rib meas 2" [5 cm] from beg.

Begin St st and cont with Color A

Next rnd: Knit with Color A.
Cont in St st until sleeve meas 2½ (2½, 2½, 3, 3, 3½, 3½)" [6.5 (6.5, 6.5, 7.5, 7.5, 9, 9) cm] from beg.

Begin sleeve shaping

Next rnd inc rnd: K2, m1-R, work to last 2 sts, m1-L, k2 (2 sts inc'd)—34 (36, 36, 38, 38, 40, 40) sts.
Rep inc rnd every 8th (12th, 12th, 16th, 16th, 16th, 14th) rnd 3 (1, 3, 3, 1, 3, 5) times, then every 6th (10th, 10th, 14th, 14th, 14th, 12th) rnd 2 (3, 1, 1, 4, 2, 1) times—44 (44, 44, 46, 48, 50, 52) sts.

Cont working even in St st until sleeve meas 8½ (9½, 10½, 13½, 15, 16, 17)" [21 5 (24, 26.5, 34.5, 38, 40.5, 43) cm] from beg, ending last rnd 3 (3, 4, 4, 4, 5, 5) sts before BOR m.

Separate for underarm

Next rnd: Sl next 6 (6, 8, 8, 8, 10, 10) sts to st holder or waste yarn, removing BOR m—38 (38, 36, 38, 40, 40, 42) sleeve sts rem. Break yarn, place rem sts onto st holder or waste yarn and set aside.

Rep for second sleeve, keeping sts on the needle at the end.

Yoke
Join sleeves to body

Next rnd: With body sts still on longer, larger circ, pm for BOR, k38 (38, 36, 38, 40, 40, 42) sleeve sts, pm for raglan, k17 (18, 18, 20, 22, 22, 24) sts for left front, pm for left front neck (use a different color than raglan), k13 (14, 15, 16, 16, 17, 17) sts for center front neck, pm for right front neck (use different color than raglan), k17 (18, 18, 20, 22, 22, 24) sts for right front, pm for raglan, k38 (38, 36, 38, 40, 40, 42) sleeve sts, pm for raglan, k47 (50, 51, 56, 60, 61, 65) back sts to end—170 (176, 174, 188, 200, 202, 214) sts.

Begin short rows and raglan shaping

Short-Row 1: (RS) Knit to left front neck m, turn.
Short-Row 2: Yo, purl to right front neck m, turn.

Short-Row 3 raglan dec row: Yo, *knit to 3 sts before raglan m, ssk, k1, sl m, k1, k2tog; rep from * three more times, knit to 4 sts before last left front neck gap (not counting yo), turn (8 sts dec'd)—162 (168, 166, 180, 192, 194, 206) sts rem.
Short-Row 4: Yo, purl to 4 sts before last right front neck gap (not counting yo), turn.
Rep Short-Rows 3 and 4 one more time (8 sts dec'd)—154 (160, 158, 172, 184, 186, 198) sts rem.
Next row raglan dec & short-row completion row: (RS) Yo, *knit to 3 sts before m, ssk, k1, sl m, k2tog: rep from * three more times, [knit across front sts to short-row yo, k2tog (yo with the following st)] 2 times, knit to left front neck m, remove m, [knit across front sts to one st before next short-row yo, ssk (next st with yo)] 2 times, knit to right front neck m, remove m, knit to end (8 sts dec'd)—146 (152, 150, 164, 176, 178, 190) sts rem; 32 (32, 30, 32, 34, 34, 36) sts each sleeve and 41 (44, 45, 50, 54, 55, 59) sts each back and front.

Cont Raglan Shaping

(Note: Change to shorter, larger circ when necessary.)
Sizes 22¼ (23½, -, 27, 28¾, 30, 31½)" only:
Next rnd raglan dec rnd: *K1, k2tog, knit to 3 sts before m, ssk, k1, sl m; rep from * three more times (8 sts dec'd)—138 (144, -, 156, 168, 170, 182) sts rem.
Rep raglan dec rnd every other rnd 0 (0, -, 0, 0, 1, 1) more times—138 (144, -, 156, 168, 162, 174) sts rem; 30 (30, -, 30, 32, 30, 32) sts each sleeve and 39 (42, 45, 48, 52, 51, 55) sts each back and front.

All Sizes:

Work 1 (1, 2, 1, 3, 4, 5) rnds even.

Re-position BOR marker

Next rnd: Remove BOR m, [knit to next m, remove m] 2 times, knit across right sleeve sts to right back raglan m. This is the new BOR.

Set up dec rnd: *K21 (22, 23, 24, 26, 25, 27) sts, k2tog; rep from * to end (6 sts dec'd)—132 (138, 144, 150, 162, 156, 168) sts rem.

Begin fair isle yoke chart

Work Rnds 1-23 of Yoke Chart (page 95), joining Colors B, C, and D as indicated by chart—88 (92, 96, 100, 108, 104, 112) sts rem.

Break Colors B, C, and D and cont in Color A only as follows:
Next rnd: Knit.

Begin final rounds of yoke shaping

Next rnd *dec rnd:* *[K3 (4, 4, 4, 3, 4, 3), k2tog] 1 (3, 1, 3, 3, 1, 2) times, [k4 (5, 5, 5, 4, 5, 4), k2tog] 1 (4, 6, 1, 2, 1, 3) times; rep from * to end—72 (78, 82, 84, 88, 88, 92) sts rem.

Change to smaller circ.

Begin 1x1 rib

Next rnd: With Color A, *k1, p1; rep from * to end. Rep the last rnd until rib meas 2 (2, 2, 2, 2½, 2½, 2½)" [5 (5, 5, 5, 6.5, 6.5, 6.5) cm] from beg.

Next rnd: BO all sts in rib pattern.

Collar

Fold rib over 1 (1, 1, 1, 1¼, 1¼, 1¼)" [2.5 (2.5, 2.5, 2.5, 3, 3, 3) cm] down and sew to WS of yoke where the 1x1 rib begins.

Finishing
Join Underarms

Turn sweater inside out. Return 6 (6, 8, 8, 8, 10, 10) held sts from one sleeve and corresponding body underarm to separate dpns, join them (with RS together) using the three-needle BO. Rep for second underarm.

Weave in ends. Wet-block to measurements.

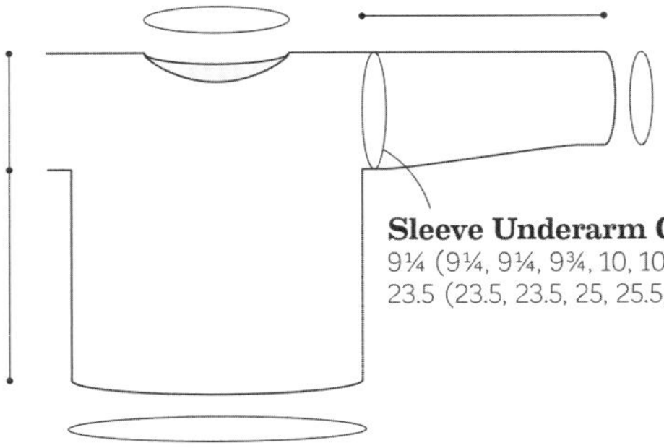

Collar Circumference
15¼ (16½, 17¼, 17¾, 18½, 18½, 19½)"
38.5 (42, 44, 45, 47, 47, 49.5) cm

Sleeve Length
8½ (9½, 10½, 13½, 15, 16, 17)"
21.5 (24, 26.5, 34.5, 38, 40.5, 43) cm

Yoke Depth
5¼ (5¼, 5¼, 5¼, 5¾, 6¼, 6½)"
20.5 (21.5, 23, 24, 26.5, 30.5, 33) cm

Sleeve Cuff Circumference
6¾ (7¼, 7¼, 7½, 7½, 8, 8)"
17 (18.5, 18.5, 19, 19, 29.5, 20.5) cm

Body Length
8 (8½, 9, 9½, 10½, 12, 13)"
20.5 (21.5, 23, 24, 26.5, 30.5, 33) cm

Sleeve Underarm Circumference
9¼ (9¼, 9¼, 9¾, 10, 10½, 11)"
23.5 (23.5, 23.5, 25, 25.5, 26.5, 28) cm

Chest Circumference
22¼ (23½, 24¾, 27, 29¾, 30, 31½)"
56.5 (59.5, 63, 68.5, 75.5, 76, 80) cm

little lighthouse chart

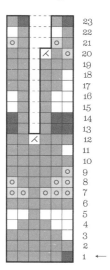

KEY

- Color A: Kumlien's Gull
- Color B: Honey
- Color C: Clay
- Color D: Bird's egg
- K2tog: Knit 2 together (with color A)

lighthouse chart

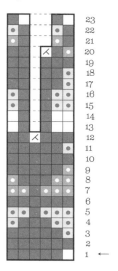

KEY

- Color A: Sabine
- Color B: Egret
- Color C: Iceland
- Color D: Kumlien's Gull
- K2tog: Knit 2 together (with color A)

lighthouse pullover
carrie bostick hoge

Finished measurements
32½ (35¾, 39¼, 42, 45, 48½, 52¼, 55¼, 57¼)" [82.5 (91, 99.5, 106.5, 114.5, 123, 132.5, 140.5, 145.5) cm] bust circumference
Shown in size 35¾" [89 cm] with ¾" [2 cm] positive ease.
Suggested ease: 0-2" [0–5 cm] positive ease

Yarn
Lark by Quince & Co. (100% American wool; 50 grams / 134 yards [123 meters])
• 6 (6, 7, 7, 8, 8, 9, 9, 10) skeins Sabine (Color A)
• 1 (1, 1, 1, 1, 1, 2, 2, 2) skeins Egret (Color B)
• 1 skein Iceland (Color C)
• 1 (1, 1, 2, 2, 2, 2, 2, 2) skeins Kumlien's Gull (Color D)
OR in worsted weight yarn:
• 694 (741, 806, 867, 937, 996, 1083, 1149, 1222) yards [635 (678, 738, 793, 857, 911, 991, 1051, 1118) meters] Color A
• 91 (97, 106, 114, 123, 131, 142, 151, 160) yards [84 (89, 97, 105, 113, 120, 130, 139, 147) meters] Color B
• 70 (74, 81, 87, 94, 100, 108, 115, 122) yards [65 (68, 75, 80, 86, 92, 99, 106, 112) meters] Color C
• 112 (120, 130, 140, 151, 161, 175, 185, 197) yards [103 (110, 119, 129, 139, 148, 161, 170, 181) meters] Color D

Needles
• One 16" [40 cm] and 32" [80 cm] circular needles (circ) in size US 7 [4.5 mm]
• One 16" [40 cm] circ in size US 6 [4 mm]
• One set of double-pointed needles (dpns) in size US 7 [4.5 mm]
Or size to obtain gauge

Notions
• Stitch markers
• Stitch holders or waste yarn
• Tapestry needle

Gauge
19 sts and 28 rnds = 4" [10 cm] in stockinette stitch with larger needles, after blocking.

Notes
On Chart Rnds 13–20, the 4th stitch has been decreased and is not worked; on Rnds 21–23, the 3rd and 4th stitches have been decreased and are not worked.

Pullover
Body
With Color A, larger, longer circ, and using the long-tail cast on, CO 158 (174, 190, 204, 218, 234, 252, 266, 276) sts. Pm for BOR and join to work in the rnd, being careful not to twist sts.

Begin 1x1 rib
First rnd: *K1, p1; rep from * to end.
Rep the last rnd until rib meas 3" [7.5 cm] from beg.

Begin St st, place markers for side, cont with Color A
Work in St st in the rnd until body meas 5" [12.5 cm] from beg.
Next rnd: K79 (87, 95, 102, 109, 117, 126, 133, 138), pm, k79 (87, 95, 102, 109, 117, 126, 133, 138) to end.

Begin side shaping, decreases
Next rnd *dec rnd:* *K2, k2tog, knit to 4 sts before next m, ssk, k2, sl m; rep from * one more time (4 sts dec'd)—154 (170, 186, 200, 214, 230, 248, 262, 272) sts rem.
Rep *dec rnd* every 10th rnd three more times—142 (158, 174, 188, 202, 218, 236, 250, 260) sts rem.

Cont working even in St st until body meas 10½" [26.5 cm] from beg.

Begin side shaping, increases

Next rnd *inc rnd:* *K2, m1-L, knit to 2 sts before next m, m1-R, k2, sl m; rep from * once more (4 sts inc'd)—146 (162, 178, 192, 206, 222, 240, 254, 264) sts. Rep *inc rnd* every 10th rnd two more times—154 (170, 186, 200, 214, 230, 248, 262, 272) sts.

Cont working even in St st until body meas 15" [38 cm] from beg.

Separate for Front and Back

Next rnd: K4 (4, 5, 5, 5, 6, 7, 7, 7), sl the last 8 (8, 10, 10, 10, 12, 14, 14, 14) sts to st holder or waste yarn removing BOR marker, knit to side m, k4 (4, 5, 5, 5, 6, 7, 7, 7), sl the last 8 (8, 10, 10, 10, 12, 14, 14, 14) sts to st holder or waste yarn, knit to end—69 (77, 83, 90, 97, 103, 110, 117, 122) sts rem for each back and front.

Keep sts on circ and set aside. Do not break yarn.

Sleeves

With Color A, dpns, and using the long-tail cast on, CO 40 (40, 42, 44, 46, 46, 48, 50, 52) sts. Pm for BOR and join to work in the rnd, being careful not to twist sts.

Begin 1x1 rib

First rnd: *K1, p1; rep from * to end.
Rep the last rnd until rib meas 3½" [9 cm] from beg.

Begin St st and cont with Color A

Next rnd: Knit with Color A.
Cont in St st until sleeve meas 4½ (4½, 4½, 4, 4, 4, 4, 4, 4)" [11.5 (11.5, 11.5, 10, 10, 10, 10, 10, 10) cm] from beg.

Begin sleeve shaping

Next rnd *inc rnd:* K2, m1-R, knit to last 2 sts, m1-L, k2 (2 sts inc'd)—42 (42, 44, 46, 48, 48, 50, 52, 54) sts. Rep *inc rnd* every 8th (6th, 6th, 6th, 6th, 4th, 4th, 4th, 4th) rnd 7 (2, 6, 10, 12, 5, 10, 11, 17) times, then every 10th (8th, 8th, 8th, 8th, 6th, 6th, 6th, 6th) rnd 2 (8, 5, 2, 1, 10, 7, 7, 3) times—60 (62, 66, 70, 74, 78, 84, 88, 94) sts.

Cont working even in St st until sleeve meas 18½" [47 cm] from beg, ending last rnd 4 (4, 5, 5, 5, 6, 7, 7, 7) sts before BOR m.

Separate for underarm

Next rnd: Sl next 8 (8, 10, 10, 10, 12, 14, 14, 14) sts to st holder or waste yarn, removing BOR m—52 (54, 56, 60, 64, 66, 70, 74, 80) sleeve sts rem. Break yarn, slip onto st holder or waste yarn yarn and set aside.

Rep for second sleeve, keeping sts on the needle at the end.

Yoke
Join sleeves to body

Next rnd: With body sts still on circ, pm for BOR, k52 (54, 56, 60, 64, 66, 70, 74, 80) sleeve sts, pm for raglan, k23 (27, 30, 33, 36, 38, 41, 44, 46) sts for left front, pm for left front neck (use different color than raglan), k23 (23, 23, 24, 25, 27, 28, 29, 30) sts for center front neck, pm for right front neck (use different color than raglan), k23 (27, 30, 33, 36, 38, 41, 44, 46) sts for right front, pm for raglan, k52 (54, 56, 60, 64, 66, 70, 74, 80) sleeve sts, pm for raglan, k69 (77, 83, 90, 97, 103, 110, 117, 122) back sts to end—242 (262, 278, 300, 322, 338, 360, 382, 404) sts.

Begin short rows and raglan shaping

(Note: Change to shorter, larger circ when necessary.)
Short-Row 1: (RS) Knit to left front neck m, turn.
Short-Row 2: Yo, purl to right front neck m, turn.
Short-Row 3 *raglan dec row:* Yo, *knit to 3 sts before m, ssk, k1, sl m, k1, k2tog; rep from * three more times, knit to 4 sts before last left front neck gap (not counting yo), turn (8 sts dec'd)—234 (254, 270, 292, 314, 330, 352, 374, 396) sts rem.
Short-Row 4: Yo, purl to 4 sts before last right front neck gap, turn.
Rep the last 2 rnds 3 (4, 4, 5, 5, 6, 6, 7, 7) more times—210 (222, 238, 252, 274, 282, 304, 318, 340) sts rem; 44 (44, 46, 48, 52, 52, 56, 58, 64) sts each sleeve and 61 (67, 73, 78, 85, 89, 96, 101, 106) sts each back and front.

Sizes 32½ (35¾, -, -, -, -, -, -, -)" only:

Next row *short-row completion row:* Yo, *knit to the first yo gap formed by short-rows, k2tog (yo with the following st); rep from * for each yo gap to the left front neck m, remove m, **knit to one st before the next yo gap (removing right front neck m as you pass it), sl that st knitwise, put it back on the left needle, then knit that st together with the following st (the yo) in the back; rep from ** until the last yo gap is closed, knit to end.

Sizes - (-, 39¼, 42, 45, 48½, 52¼, 55¼, 57¼)" only:

Next row *raglan dec & short-row completion row:* (RS) Yo, *knit to 3 sts before m, ssk, k1, sl m, k2tog: rep from * three more times, [knit across front sts to short-row yo, k2tog (yo with the following st)] - (-, 5, 6, 6, 7, 7, 8, 8) times, knit to left front neck m, remove m, [knit across front sts to one st before next short-row yo, ssk (next st with yo)] - (-, 5, 6, 6, 7, 7, 8, 8) times, knit to right front neck m, remove m, knit to end (8 sts dec'd)— - (-, 230, 244, 266, 274, 296, 310, 332) sts rem.

97

Cont Raglan Shaping

Next rnd: Knit.

Next rnd raglan dec rnd: *K1, k2tog, knit to 3 sts before m, ssk, k1, sl m; rep from * three more times (8 sts dec'd)— - (-, 222, 236, 258, 266, 288, 302, 324) sts rem. Rep *raglan dec rnd* every other rnd - (-, 0, 1, 3, 4, 6, 7, 9) more times— - (-, 222, 228, 234, 234, 240, 246, 252) sts rem; - (-, 42, 42, 42, 40, 40, 40, 42) sts each sleeve and - (-, 69, 72, 75, 77, 80, 83, 84) sts each back and front.

All Sizes:

Re-position BOR marker

Next row: Remove BOR m, [knit to next m, remove m] 2 times, knit across right sleeve sts to right back raglan m. This is the new BOR.

Next rnd: Knit.

Set up dec rnd: *K33 (35, 35, 36, 37, 37, 38, 39, 40), k2tog; rep from * to end (6 sts dec'd)—204 (216, 216, 222, 228, 228, 234, 240, 246) sts rem.

Begin Chart for yoke fair isle

Work Rnds 1-23 of Yoke Chart (page 95), joining Colors B, C, and D as indicated by chart—136 (144, 144, 148, 152, 152, 156, 160, 164) sts rem.

Break Colors B, C, and D and cont in Color A only as follows:

Next rnd: Knit.

Begin final rounds of yoke shaping

Next rnd dec rnd: *K2, k2tog; rep from * to end— 102 (108, 108, 111, 114, 114, 117, 120, 123) sts rem.

Next rnd dec rnd: K0 (0, 0, 3, 0, 0, 3, 0, 3), *k2tog, k4; rep from * to end—85 (90, 90, 93, 95, 95, 98, 100, 103) sts rem.

Change to smaller circ.

Sizes 32½ (-, -, 42, 45, 48½, -, -, 57¼)" only:

Next rnd dec rnd: With Color A, k2tog, knit to end— 84 (-, -, 92, 94, 94, -, -, 102) sts rem.

Sizes - (35¾, 39¼, -, -, -, 52¼, 55¼, -)" only:

Next rnd: With Color A, knit to end.

All Sizes:

Begin 1x1 rib

Next rnd: With Color A, *k1, p1; rep from * to end. Rep the last rnd until rib meas 2½" [6.5 cm] from beg.

Next rnd: BO all sts in rib pattern.

Collar

Fold rib over 1¼" [3 cm] down and sew to WS of yoke where the 1x1 rib begins.

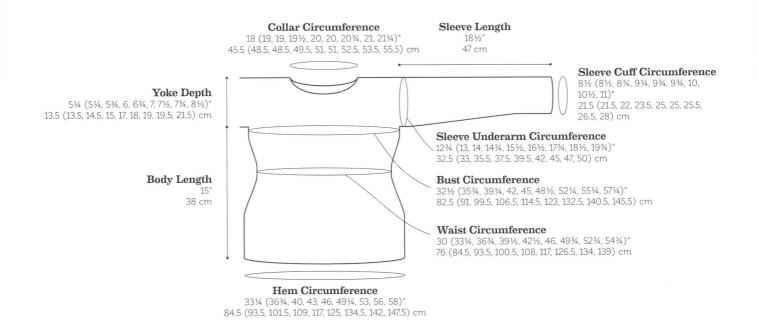

Collar Circumference
18 (19, 19, 19½, 20, 20, 20¾, 21, 21¾)"
45.5 (48.5, 48.5, 49.5, 51, 51, 52.5, 53.5, 55.5) cm

Sleeve Length
18½"
47 cm

Sleeve Cuff Circumference
8½ (8½, 8¾, 9¼, 9¾, 9¾, 10, 10½, 11)"
21.5 (21.5, 22, 23.5, 25, 25, 25.5, 26.5, 28) cm

Yoke Depth
5¼ (5¼, 5¾, 6, 6¾, 7, 7½, 7¾, 8½)"
13.5 (13.5, 14.5, 15, 17, 18, 19, 19.5, 21.5) cm

Sleeve Underarm Circumference
12¾ (13, 14, 14¾, 15½, 16½, 17¾, 18½, 19¾)"
32.5 (33, 35.5, 37.5, 39.5, 42, 45, 47, 50) cm

Body Length
15"
38 cm

Bust Circumference
32½ (35¾, 39¼, 42, 45, 48½, 52¼, 55¼, 57¼)"
82.5 (91, 99.5, 106.5, 114.5, 123, 132.5, 140.5, 145.5) cm

Waist Circumference
30 (33¼, 36¾, 39½, 42½, 46, 49¾, 52¾, 54¾)"
76 (84.5, 93.5, 100.5, 108, 117, 126.5, 134, 139) cm

Hem Circumference
33¼ (36¾, 40, 43, 46, 49¼, 53, 56, 58)"
84.5 (93.5, 101.5, 109, 117, 125, 134.5, 142, 147.5) cm

Finishing
Join Underarms
Turn sweater inside out. Return 8 (8, 10, 10, 10, 12, 14, 14, 14) held sts from one sleeve and corresponding body underarm to separate dpns, join them (with RS together) using the three-needle BO. Rep for second underarm.

Weave in ends. Wet-block to measurements.

camp cap
carrie bostick hoge

Finished measurements
16½ (18¾, 21)" [41.5 (47, 53) cm]
To fit: Toddler (Kid, Woman)

Yarn
The All American Collection by Swans Island
(75% American wool, 25% American Alpaca;
80 grams / 210 yards [192 meters])
• 1 skein, shown in Frost (Toddler), Lichen (Babe &
woman), and Pomegranate (woman)
OR
75 (100, 125) yards [69 (92, 115) meters] in heavy
worsted weight yarn

Needles
• One 16" [40 cm] circular needle (circ) in size US 7
  [4.5 mm]
  Toddler hat will only use dpns
• One set double-pointed needles (dpns) in size US 7
  [4.5 mm]
Or size to obtain gauge

Notions
• Stitch marker
• Tapestry needle

Gauge
17 sts and 27 rnds= 4" [10 cm] in broken rib,
after blocking.

Cap
Using the long-tail cast on, CO 70 (80, 90) sts, pm for
BOR, being careful not to twist sts.

Begin Broken rib
Rnd 1: *K1, p1; rep from * to end.
Rnd 2: Knit.
Cont in patt until cap meas 3½ (3¾, 5)" [9 (9.5, 12.5)
cm] from beg, ending after Rnd 1.

Begin garter st crown
Next rnd: Purl.
Next rnd: Knit.
Next rnd: Purl.

Begin Crown Shaping
Rnd 1 *dec rnd:* *K2tog, k8; rep from * to end [7 (8, 9 sts
dec'd each dec rnd)]—63 (72, 81) sts.
Rnd 2 and all even rnds: Purl.
Rnd 3 *dec rnd:* *K2tog, k7; rep from * to end—56 (64,
72) sts.
Rnd 5 *dec rnd:* *K2tog, k6; rep from * to end—49 (56,
63) sts.
Rnd 7 *dec rnd:* *K2tog, k5; rep from * to end—42 (48,
54) sts.

Rnd 9 *dec rnd:* *K2tog, k4; rep from * to end—35 (40,
45) sts.
Rnd 11 *dec rnd:* *K2tog, k3; rep from * to end—28 (32,
36) sts.
Rnd 13 *dec rnd:* *K2tog, k2; rep from * to end—21 (24,
27) sts.
Rnd 15 *dec rnd:* *K2tog, k1; rep from * to end—14 (16,
18) sts.
Rnd 17 *dec rnd:* *K2tog; rep from * to end—7 (8, 9) sts.

For sizes 16½ (-, 21)" only:
Rnd 19 *dec rnd:* *K2tog; rep from * to last st, k1
[3 (-, 4 sts dec'd)]—4 (-, 5) sts rem.
Rnd 18: Purl.

For - (18¾, -)" only
Rnd 19 *dec rnd:* *K2tog; rep from * to end (4 sts
dec'd)—4 sts.

Finishing
Break yarn and thread onto tapestry needle. Draw
through rem sts and cinch closed. Make pom-pom and
attach to top, if desired.
Weave in ends. Block to measurements.

conifer cowl
carrie bostick hoge

Finished measurements
8" [20.5 cm] wide, 56" [142 cm] long

Yarn
The All American Collection by Swans Island
(75% American wool, 25% American Alpaca;
80 grams / 210 yards [192 meters])
• 2 skeins in Conifer
OR
350 yards [320 meters] in heavy worsted weight yarn

Needles
• One pair of straight needles in size US 7 [4.5 mm]
Or size to obtain gauge

Notions
• Tapestry needle

Gauge
17 sts and 28 rows = 4" [10 cm] in garter stitch rib,
after blocking.

Cowl
Using the provisional cast on, CO 34 sts.

Begin garter stitch rib
First row: (WS) K2, *p2, k2; rep from * to end.
Next row: (RS) Knit.
Rep the last 2 rows until cowl meas 56" [142 cm] from
beg, ending after a WS row.

Remove waste yarn from provisional cast-on and place
34 sts onto spare needle. Using the three-needle
bindoff, join beginning of cowl to end of cowl, being
careful not to twist.

Finishing
Weave in ends. Wet block to measurements.

sunrise cardi

cecily glowik macdonald

Early morning Maine skies are so colorful and put me right at ease. To pay homage to these moments, I created this cocoon cardi with its soft, textured fabric and easy to wear, relaxed style.

Finished measurements
39½ (47, 53, 59½, 67, 75, 81½)" [100.5 (119.5, 134.5, 151, 170, 190.5, 207) cm] body circumference (see Notes)
To Fit: 35¼ (39½, 43, 45¾, 50¾, 54¾, 59)" [89.5 (100.5, 109, 116, 129, 139, 150) cm] bust circumference
Shown in size to fit 35¼" [89.5 cm] with 1" [2.5 cm] positive ease.
Suggested ease: 1-3" [2.5–7.5 cm] of positive ease

Yarn
Tern by Quince and Co. (75% American Wool, 25% Silk; 50 grams / 221 yds [202 meters])
• 5 (6, 7, 8, 9, 10, 11) skeins in Iron
OR 1017 (1254, 1404, 1579, 1816, 2048, 2221) yards [930 (1147, 1284, 1444, 1661, 1873, 2031) meters] in fingering weight yarn

Needles
• One 32" [80 cm] circular needle (circ) in size US 6 [4 mm]
• One set of double-pointed needles (dpns) in size US 6 [4 mm]
Or size to obtain gauge

Notions
• Stitch holders or waste yarn
• Tapestry needle

Gauge
23 sts and 35 rows = 4" [10 cm] in Texture Pattern, after blocking.

Texture Pattern: (multiple of 2 sts + 1)
Row 1: (RS) Knit.
Row 2: (WS) Purl.
Row 3: *K1, p1; rep from * to last st, k1.
Row 4: Purl.
Rep Rows 1–4 for patt.

Notes
There is extra circumference on the body of the sweater to provide the necessary space for your upper arms. Choose the size you make to match the "to fit" measurements.
Circular needle is used to accommodate large number of sts. Do not join; work back and forth in rows.

Cardi
Body
With circ and using the long-tail cast on, CO 190 (234, 262, 298, 342, 382, 418) sts. Do not join.

Begin 2x2 Rib
First row: (WS) *P2, k2; rep from * to last 2 sts, p2.
Next row: (RS) *K2, p2; rep from * to last 2 sts, k2.
Cont working in 2x2 rib as est until piece meas 1¼" [3 cm] from beg, ending after a RS row.

Next row *purl ridge and dec row:* (WS) K2tog, [k0 (76, 0, 97, 112, 125, 137), k2tog] 0 (2, 0, 2, 2, 2, 2) times, knit to end—189 (231, 261, 295, 339, 379, 415) sts rem.

Begin Texture Pattern
Next row: (RS) Work Texture Patt to end.
Cont working even in Texture Patt until piece meas 10¼ (10, 9¾, 9½, 9¼, 9, 8½)" [26 (25.5, 25, 24, 23.5, 23, 21.5) cm] from CO edge, ending after a WS row.

Separate for Fronts and Back
Next row: (RS) Work 38 (48, 54, 62, 73, 82, 90) sts as est, transfer sts just worked to waste yarn or st holder for right front, work 113 (135, 153, 171, 193, 215, 235) sts, transfer sts just worked to a second waste yarn or st holder for back, work rem 38 (38, 54, 62, 73, 82, 90) sts for left front. Cont working back and forth in rows on left front sts only.

Left Front
Cont working as est until piece meas 5 (5½, 6, 6½, 7, 7½, 8)" [12.5 (14, 15, 16.5, 18, 19, 20.5) cm] from separate for fronts and back, ending after a WS row.

Shape Side/Sleeves
Next row *side dec row:* (RS) K2, ssk, work to end (1 st dec'd)—37 (47, 53, 61, 72, 81, 89) sts rem.
Rep *side dec row* every 4th row 4 (4, 2, 0, 0, 0, 0) more times, then every other row 15 (20, 26, 30, 32, 33, 33) times—18 (23, 25, 31, 40, 48, 56) sts rem.

Sizes 35¼ (39½, 43, -, -, -, -)" only:
Work 1 WS row even.

Sizes - (-, -, 45¾, 50¾, 54¾, 59)" only:
Next row WS *side dec row:* (WS) Work to last 4 sts, ssp, p2 (1 st dec'd)— - (-, -, 30, 39, 47, 55) sts rem.
Next row: (RS) Rep *side dec row* (1 st dec'd)— - (-, -, 29, 38, 46, 54) sts rem.
Rep the last 2 rows - (-, -, 0, 1, 3, 5) more times, then work one more WS *side dec row*— - (-, -, 28, 35, 39, 43) sts rem.

All Sizes:
BO for Shoulder
Row 1: (RS) BO 4 (5, 5, 7, 8, 9, 10) sts, work to end— 14 (18, 20, 21, 27, 30, 33) sts rem.
Row 2: (WS) Work even as est.
Row 3: BO 4 (6, 6, 7, 9, 10, 11) sts, work to end—10 (12, 14, 14, 18, 20, 22) sts rem.
Row 4: Rep Row 2.
Row 5: BO 5 (6, 7, 7, 9, 10, 11) sts, work to end [5 (6, 7, 7, 9, 10, 11) sts dec'd]—6 (6, 7, 7, 9, 10, 11) sts rem.
Rep Rows 4 and 5 one more time.

Right Front
Transfer 38 (48, 54, 62, 73, 82, 90) held right front sts to circ needle and join yarn ready to work a WS row.

Cont working even as est until piece meas 5 (5½, 6, 6½, 7, 7½, 8)" [12.5 (14, 15, 16.5, 18, 19, 20.5) cm] from separation for fronts and back, ending after a WS row.

Shape Side/Sleeve
Next row *side dec row:* (RS) Work to last 4 sts, k2tog, k2 (1 st dec'd)—37 (47, 53, 61, 72, 81, 89) sts rem.
Rep *side dec row* every 4th row 4 (4, 2, 0, 0, 0, 0) more times, then every other row 15 (20, 26, 30, 32, 33, 33) times—18 (23, 25, 31, 40, 48, 56) sts rem.

Sizes 35¼ (39½, 43, -, -, -, -)" only:
Work 2 rows even, ending after a RS Row.

Sizes - (-, -, 45¾, 50¾, 54¾, 59)" only:
Next row WS *side dec row:* (WS) P2, k2tog, work to end (1 st dec'd)— - (-, -, 30, 39, 47, 55) sts rem.
Next row: (RS) Rep *side dec row* (1 st dec'd)— - (-, -, 29, 38, 46, 54) sts rem.
Rep the last 2 rows - (-, -, 0, 1, 3, 5) more times, then work one more WS *side dec row*— - (-, -, 28, 35, 39, 43) sts rem.
Next row: (RS) Work even as est.

All Sizes:
BO for Shoulder
Row 1: (WS) BO 4 (5, 5, 7, 8, 9, 10) sts, work to end— 14 (18, 20, 21, 27, 30, 33) sts rem.
Row 2: (RS) Work even as est.
Row 3: BO 4 (6, 6, 7, 9, 10, 11) sts, work to end—10 (12, 14, 14, 18, 20, 22) sts rem.
Row 4: Rep Row 2.
Row 5: BO 5 (6, 7, 7, 9, 10, 11) sts, work to end [5 (6, 7, 7, 9, 10, 11) sts dec'd]—5 (6, 7, 7, 9, 10, 11) sts rem.
Rep Rows 4 and 5 one more time.

Back
Transfer 113 (135, 153, 171, 193, 215, 235) held back sts to circ and join yarn ready to work a WS row.

Cont working even as est until piece meas 5 (5½, 6, 6½, 7, 7½, 8)" [12.5 (14, 15, 16.5, 18, 19, 20.5) cm] from separation for fronts and back, ending after a WS row.

Shape Sides/Sleeves
Next row *side dec row:* (RS) K2, ssk, work to last 4 sts, k2tog, k2 (2 sts dec'd)—111 (133, 151, 169, 191, 213, 233) sts rem.

Rep *side dec row* every 4th row 4 (4, 2, 0, 0, 0, 0) more times then every other row 15 (20, 26, 30, 32, 33, 33) times—73 (85, 95, 109, 127, 147, 167) sts rem.

Sizes 35¼ (39½, 43, -, -, -, -)" only:
Work 1 WS row even.

Sizes - (-, -, 45¾, 50¾, 54¾, 59)" only:
Next row WS *side dec row:* (WS) P2, p2tog, work to last 4 sts, ssp, p2 (2 sts dec'd)— - (-, -, 107, 125, 145, 165) sts rem.
Next row: (RS) Rep *side dec row* (2 sts dec'd)— - (-, -, 105, 123, 143, 163) sts rem.
Rep the last 2 rows - (-, -, 0, 1, 3, 5) more times, then work one more WS *side dec row*— - (-, -, 103, 117, 129, 141) sts rem.

All Sizes:
BO for Shoulder
BO 4 (5, 5, 7, 8, 9, 10) sts at the beg of the next 2 rows, BO 4 (6, 6, 7, 9, 10, 11) sts at the beg of the following 2 rows, then BO 5 (6, 7, 7, 9, 10, 11) sts at the beg of the next 4 rows—37 (39, 45, 47, 47, 51, 55) sts rem.

Next row: BO rem sts for back neck.

Finishing
Steam- or wet-block to measurements.

Seam
Beg at first *side dec row*, seam front side/sleeve seams and shoulders to back. (Note: this leaves the 5 (5½, 6, 6½, 7, 7½, 8)" [12.5 (14, 15, 16.5, 18, 19, 20.5) cm] worked after the Separate for Fronts and Back open for armholes.)

Armhole Trim

With RS facing and dpns, beg at bottom of armhole opening, pick up and knit 60 (64, 68, 76, 80, 88, 92) sts evenly around armhole opening, pm for BOR and join to work in the rnd.

Begin 2x2 Rib

Next rnd: *K2, p2; rep from * around.
Cont working in rib as est until trim meas 1¼" [3 cm] from pick-up rnd.
Next rnd: BO all sts in pattern.
Rep for second armhole.

Collar

With RS facing and circ, beg at CO edge of right front, pick up and knit 134 (143, 148, 151, 157, 163, 167) sts up right front, 36 (38, 44, 46, 46, 50, 54) sts along back neck and 134 (143, 148, 151, 157, 163, 167) sts down left front—304 (324, 340, 348, 360, 376, 388) sts.
Next row *purl ridge row:* (WS) Knit all sts.

Begin 2x2 Rib:

Next row: (RS) K3, *p2, k2; rep form * to last st, k1.
Next row: (WS) P1, *p2, k2; rep from * to last 3 sts, p3.
Cont working in rib as est until collar meas 2¼" [5.5 cm] from pick-up row.

Next row: Loosely BO all sts in pattern.

Weave in ends. Block again if desired.

About the designer:

Cecily lives in beautiful Portland, Maine. She spends her time knitting, designing, and enjoying the wonderful hiking trails, coastline, restaurants, and the lovely people of Maine. She is the author of *Landing* and the co-author of *New England Knits* and *Weekend Hats*.

You can find her on Instagram and Twitter as cecilyam

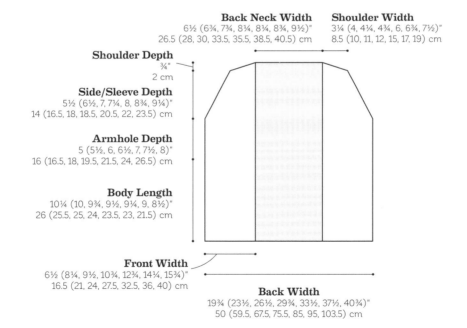

Back Neck Width
6½ (6¾, 7¾, 8¼, 8¼, 8¾, 9½)"
26.5 (28, 30, 33.5, 35.5, 38.5, 40.5) cm

Shoulder Width
3¼ (4, 4¼, 4¾, 6, 6¾, 7½)"
8.5 (10, 11, 12, 15, 17, 19) cm

Shoulder Depth
¾"
2 cm

Side/Sleeve Depth
5½ (6½, 7, 7¼, 8, 8¾, 9¼)"
14 (16.5, 18, 18.5, 20.5, 22, 23.5) cm

Armhole Depth
5 (5½, 6, 6½, 7, 7½, 8)"
16 (16.5, 18, 19.5, 21.5, 24, 26.5) cm

Body Length
10¼ (10, 9¾, 9½, 9¼, 9, 8½)"
26 (25.5, 25, 24, 23.5, 23, 21.5) cm

Front Width
6½ (8¼, 9½, 10¾, 12¾, 14¼, 15¾)"
16.5 (21, 24, 27.5, 32.5, 36, 40) cm

Back Width
19¾ (23½, 26½, 29¾, 33½, 37½, 40¾)"
50 (59.5, 67.5, 75.5, 85, 95, 103.5) cm

tree shawl

leila raabe

It's hard to beat a project that begins with the maximum number of stitches and reduces down to a single stitch to fasten off. I've always been fascinated with the botanical patterns possible in knitting, and always seek out ways to work another leaf or tree motif to a simple shape. Knitting in a versatile sport weight yarn like Chickadee results in a lightweight but warm accessory to snuggle into without too much weight or bulk.

Finished measurements

64" [162.5 cm] wingspan and 34" [86.5 cm] deep, after blocking

Yarn

Chickadee by Quince & Co. (100% American Wool; 50 grams / 181 yards [165 meters])

• 5 skeins in Audouin

OR

905 yards [825 meters] in sport weight yarn

Needles

• One 32" [80 cm] circular needle (circ) in size US 6 [4 mm]

Or size to obtain gauge

Notions

• Tapestry needle

• T-pins and blocking wires (optional, but recommended)

Gauge

19 sts and 29 rows = 4" [10 cm] in Chart A, after blocking.

Notes

• This shawl begins at the top edge with a simple double-yarnover detail, which also lays the foundation for the side edge borders that are continued all the way to the bottom point. A traditional tree lace motif is repeated throughout the center, with shaping decreases on each end that gradually whittles away the stitch count. The repeat is easy to memorize and keep track of during the project, with a single WS row that features decreases to align with the lace itself.

• The first and last stitch are kept in garter stitch throughout.

• Circular needle is used to accommodate large number of sts. Do not join; work back and forth in rows.

Shawl

Using the cable cast on, CO 306 sts. Do not join.

Begin Border

Row 1: (RS) Knit all sts.

Row 2: (WS) K1, purl to last st, k1.

Row 3 *eyelet row:* K1, *k2tog, yo twice, ssk; rep from * to last st, k1.

Row 4: K1, *p2, p1-tbl into second yo, p1; rep from * to last st, k1.

Row 5 *inc row:* K153, m1, knit to end (1 st inc'd)—307 sts.

Row 6: K1, purl to last st, k1.

Begin Charts
Notes on charts:
• Shawl decreases occur inside the double-yarnover borders throughout.
• Stitch count decreases by 2 sts every RS row.
Stitch count decreases by a further 2 sts on WS row 10.
A total of 12 sts are decreased for each 10-row repeat.

Begin Lace Chart A
Work Rows 1–10 of Lace Chart A 23 times—31 sts rem.

Begin Lace Chart B
Work Rows 1–10 of Lace Chart B once—19 sts rem.

Begin Lace Chart C
Work Rows 1–8 of Lace Chart C once—9 sts rem.

Begin Lace Chart D
Work Rows 1–5 of Lace Chart D once—3 sts rem.

Next row: (WS) K3tog (2 sts dec'd)—1 st rem.

Break yarn and draw through final st, fastening off.

Finishing
Weave in ends. Wet-block to measurements.

About the designer:

Leila lives in Portland, Maine, a beautiful city comprised of equal parts plaid and brick. Currently stationed at Quince & Co, she wishes there were more design hours to be utilized in any given day. Find out what she's up to these days at leilaknits.com.

tree shawl

CHART D

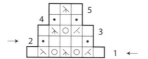

CHART C

CHART B

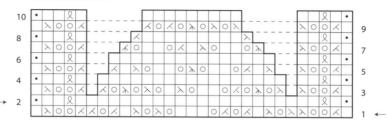

CHART A

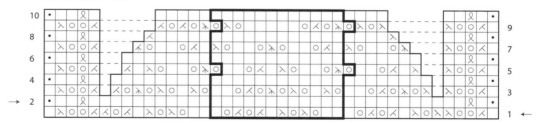

KEY

☐	Knit on RS; Purl on WS
•	Purl on RS; Knit on WS
○	YO: Yarn over (1 st increased)
↘	SSK (RS): Slip, slip, knit; SSP (WS): Slip, slip, purl (1 st decreased; leans left on RS)
↗	K2tog (RS): Knit 2 together; P2tog (WS) - Purl 2 together (1 st decreased; leans right)
↑	SK2P: Slip 1 st as if to knit, k2tog, pass slipped st over (2 sts decreased; leans left)
⋏	K3tog: Knit 3 together (2 sts decreased; leans right)
ℓ	P1tbl: Purl through the back loop, twisting the stitch

109

lichen mittens

mary jane mucklestone

Inspired by the yellow lichen on granite rocks found in coastal Maine. Especially, my favorite rock from Nash Island, Maine.

Finished measurements
7¼" [18.5 cm] hand circumference, 9¾" [25 cm] long

Yarn
Lark by Quince & Co. (100% American wool; 50 grams / 134 yards [123 meters])
• 2 skeins in Kittywake (MC)
• 1 skein in Honey (CC)
OR in worsted weight yarn:
• 150 yards [137 meters] MC
• 60 yards [55 meters] CC

Needles
• One set of double-pointed needles (dpns) in size US 4 [3.5mm] and US 5 [3.75mm]
Or size to obtain gauge

Notions
• Locking stitch marker
• Waste yarn
• Tapestry needle

Gauge
20 sts and 26 rnds = 4" [10 cm] in Colorwork Chart, after blocking.

Note
On colorwork rounds, tack down the CC float on the 3rd MC stitch, creating shorter floats.

Mittens
With smaller dpns, MC, and using the long-tail cast on, CO 36 sts. Divide sts evenly onto 3 dpns. Place a locking st marker into first st to mark beg of rnd (BOR) and join to work in the rnd, careful not to twist sts. Knit 3 rnds.

Begin corrugated rib
Next rnd: With MC k1, with CC k1; rep from * to end.
Next rnd: With MC k1, with CC p1; rep from *.
Rep the last rnd until cuff meas 2½" [6.25 cm] from beg of rib. Break CC.
Next rnd: Knit.
Next rnd *inc rnd*: *K6, m1; rep from * to end (6 sts inc'd)—42 sts.
Place 21 sts onto 1 dpn for back of hand and divide rem sts onto 2 dpns for palm.

Change to larger dpns.
Next rnd: Knit.

Begin Colorwork Chart
Next rnd: Work Rnd 1 of Colorwork Chart to end.
Cont as est until Rnds 1-8 have been worked one time then work Rnds 1-7 one more time.

Thumb placement
Left mitten
Next rnd: Work Rnd 8 of chart to last 9 sts, sl next 8 sts onto st holder or waste yarn, using the backward loop cast on, CO 8 sts, k1.

Right mitten
Next rnd: Work Rnd 8 of chart for 22 sts, sl next 8 sts onto st holder or waste yarn, using the backward loop cast on, CO 8 sts, k1.

Continue mitten
Next rnd: Work Rnd 1 of chart to end.
Cont as est until piece meas approx 8½" [21.5 cm] from beg, ending after Rnd 3 or 7.

Begin top shaping

Note: Cont working in chart until 22 sts rem, working CC sts only when they occur at least 3 sts from a decrease.

Next rnd *dec rnd:* Ssk, knit to last 2 sts on 1st needle, k2tog; ssk, knit to last 2 sts on 3rd needle, k2tog (4 sts dec'd)—38 sts rem.

Rep *dec rnd* every rnd six more times—14 sts rem. Place sts from 2nd and 3rd dpns onto one needle. Break yarn leaving a 12" [30.5 cm] tail. Graft top using kitchener stitch.

Thumb

With MC, pick up and knit 8 sts from CO edge at top of thumb opening, place held sts evenly onto 2 dpns, then knit across—16 sts on needles.

Next rnd: Knit.

Knit every rnd until thumb meas 2" [5 cm] from pick-up rnd.

Shape thumb top

Next rnd *dec rnd:* Ssk, knit to last 2 sts on first needle, k2tog; ssk, knit to last 2 sts on 3rd needle, k2tog (4 sts dec'd)—12 sts rem.

Rep *dec rnd* every rnd two more times—4 sts rem.

Break yarn and thread onto tapestry needle. Draw through rem sts and cinch closed.

Finishing

Weave in ends taking special care where the thumb joins the body of the mitt, snugging things up a bit. Wet-block mitts to finished measurements.

lichen mittens

colorwork chart

KEY

- ■ MC: Kittywake
- ☐ CC: Honey
- ⊡ Purl

About the designer:

It was when **Mary Jane** moved to Maine 25 years ago that she found she couldn't stop knitting. With a limited budget and babies, she discovered that she could make beautiful colorful knitwear from the odd balls she found in her local yarn shop's sale bin. Mary Jane eventually published books on the subject, *200 Fair Isle Motifs, 150 Scandinavian Motifs,* and *Fair Isle Style*. She travels the world teaching knitting but is always happy to come home to Maine and stay put!

Follow her adventures on instagram @mjmucklestone and her website MaryJaneMucklestone.com

abbreviations

approx: approximately
beg: begin(ning)
BO: bind off
BOR: beginning of round
circ: circular
CC: contrasting color
cn: cable needle
CO: cast on
cont: continue
dec('d): decrease(d)
dpns: double-pointed needles
est: establish(ed)
inc('d): increase(d)
k: knit
k1-f/b: Knit into front and back of next st (1 st increased).
k2tog: Knit 2 sts together (1 st decreased).
k3tog: Knit 3 sts together (2 sts decreased, leans to the right).
LH: left hand
m: marker
MC: main color
m1 (make 1): Insert LH needle from front to back under horizontal strand between st just worked and next st, knit lifted strand through the back loop (1 st increased).
m1-L (make 1 left slanting): Insert LH needle from front to back under horizontal strand between st just worked and next st, knit lifted strand through the back loop (1 st increased).
m1-LP (make 1 left purlwise): Insert LH needle under horizontal strand between st just worked and next st from the back to the front, purl through the back loop.
m1-R (make 1 right slanting): Insert LH needle from back to front under horizontal strand between st just worked and next st, knit lifted strand through the front loop (1 st increased).

m1-RP (make 1 right purlwise): Insert LH needle under horizontal strand between st just worked and next st from the front to the back, purl through the front loop.
meas: measure(s)
p: purl
patt: pattern
p1-f/b (purl 1, front and back): Purl into the front loop, then the back loop of next st (1 st increased).
p2tog: Purl 2 sts together (1 st decreased).
pc(s): piece(s)
pm: place marker
rem: remain
rep: repeat
rnd(s): round(s)
RH: right hand
RS: right side
sl: slip
ssk (slip, slip, knit): Slip 2 sts one at a time knitwise to the RH needle; return sts to LH needle in turned position and knit them together through the back loops (1 st decreased).
ssp (slip, slip, purl): Slip 2 sts one at a time knitwise to the RH needle; return sts to LH needle in turned position and purl them together through the back loops (1 st decreased).
st(s): stitch(es)
St st: stockinette stitch
tbl: through the back loop
WS: wrong side
yo: yarn over

Backward loop cast on

*Wrap yarn around left thumb from front to back and secure in palm with other fingers. Insert needle upwards through strand on thumb. Slip loop from thumb onto RH needle, pulling yarn to tighten; rep from * for indicated number of sts.

Long tail cast on

http://www.knitty.com/ISSUEsummer05/FEAT-sum05TT.html

Provisional cast on

http://www.knitty.com/ISSUEfall05/FEATfall05TT.html

Cable cast on

Begin with a slipknot, k1 keeping slipknot on left needle, slip new st onto LH needle; *insert RH needle between first 2 sts on LH needle, k1 from this position, leave the first st on LH needle and slip new st onto LH needle; rep from * for desired number of sts.

Stockinette stitch flat

Knit on RS, purl on WS.

Stockinette stitch in the rnd

Knit every rnd.

Garter stitch flat

Knit every row.

Garter stitch in the rnd

Rnd 1: Purl.
Rnd 2: Knit.
Rep Rnds 1 and 2 for garter st in the rnd.

Kitchener stitch

http://www.knitty.com/ISSUEsummer04/FEATtheresasum04.html

Sunday Short Rows

http://www.sundayknits.com/techniques/shortrows.html

Three-needle bind off

Divide sts evenly over 2 needles; with the RS of garment pcs together (to form ridge on inside of garment), hold the needles parallel. With a third needle knit the first st of front and back needles together, *knit next st from each needle together, (2 sts on RH needle), BO 1 st; rep from * until all sts are BO.

thank you

The knitters: A *special* thank you to Sue Macurdy, you know why. Also, Nicole Dupuis, Larisa Norman, Ann Kearsley, Adi Kehoe, Aimee Chapman, Nancy Miller, Sierra Roberts, and Sommer Roberts.

The tech editors: Kristen TenDyke & Dawn Catanzaro. And thank you for proof reading Dawn and Bristol Ivy!

The charts & schematics: Leila Raabe.

The models: Imogen, Sigrid, Chloe, Meghan, and Kate.

The locations: Maine, thank you for being so incredible. The locations I photographed for this book are my favorite spots. Places I travel on a regular basis and places I have used many times as locations. I felt like it was important to pay tribute to these areas I usually frequent. If ever there is a second book...well, there are many more places here to explore!

about

Carrie Bostick Hoge is a knitwear designer and photographer living in in Maine with her husband and two daughters. She is the self-published author of the *Madder Anthology* pattern book series. Carrie's designs have also been published in Amirisu, Brooklyn Tweed's *Wool People*, *New England Knits*, *Fair Isle Style*, Interweave Knits, Knitscene, Taproot Magazine, and on Quince & Co.'s website.

www.maddermade.com